ARCHITECTURE
GOTHIC AND RENAISSANCE

LECTOR HOUSE PUBLIC DOMAIN WORKS

ARCHITECTURE GOTHIC AND RENAISSANCE

THOMAS ROGER SMITH, EDWARD JOHN POYNTER

ISBN: 978-93-89701-28-9

Published: 1880

LECTOR HOUSE LLP
E-MAIL: lectorpublishing@gmail.com

P. 97

THE CERTOSA, NEAR PAVIA. FROM THE CLOISTERS.

Begun by Marco di Campione, A.D. 1393.

ARCHITECTURE
GOTHIC AND RENAISSANCE

BY

T. ROGER SMITH, F.R.I.B.A.

Occasional Lecturer on Architecture at University College, London

TEXT-BOOK OF ART EDUCATION,
EDITED BY EDWARD J. POYNTER, R.A.

SAINT GEORGE. PANEL FROM THE TOMB OF CARDINAL AM-
BOISE IN ROUEN CATHEDRAL

1880

PREFACE.

THE history, the features, and the most famous examples of European architecture, during a period extending from the rise of the Gothic, or pointed, style in the twelfth century to the general depression which overtook the Renaissance style at the close of the eighteenth, form the subject of this little volume. I have endeavoured to adopt as free and simple a mode of treatment as is compatible with the accurate statement of at least the outlines of so very technical a subject.

Though it is to be hoped that many professional students of architecture will find this hand-book serviceable to them in their elementary studies, it has been my principal endeavour to adapt it to the requirements of those who are preparing for the professional pursuit of the sister arts, and of that large and happily increasing number of students who pursue the fine arts as a necessary part of a complete liberal education, and who know that a solid and comprehensive acquaintance with art, especially if joined to some skill in the use of the pencil, the brush, the modelling tool, or the etching needle, will open sources of pleasure and interest of the most refined description.

The broad facts of all art history; the principles which underlie each of the fine arts; and the most precious or most noteworthy examples of each, ought to be familiar to every art student, whatever special branch he may follow. Beyond these limits I have not attempted to carry this account of Gothic and Renaissance architecture; within them I have endeavoured to make the work as complete as the space at my disposal permitted.

Some portions of the text formed part of two courses of lectures delivered before the students of the School of Military Engineering at Chatham, and are introduced here by the kind permission of Sir John Stokes. Many of the descriptive and critical remarks are transcripts of notes made by myself, almost under the shadow of the buildings to which they refer. It would, however, have been impossible to give a condensed view of so extended a subject had not every part of it been treated at much greater length by previous writers. The number and variety of the books consulted renders it impossible to make any other acknowledgment here than this general recognition of my indebtedness to their authors.

T. R. S.

CONTENTS

* 2. Northern Europe 95

LIST OF ILLUSTRATIONS

ILLUSTRATED GLOSSARY
OF TECHNICAL WORDS.

ABACUS.—The upper portion of the capital of a column, upon which the weight to be carried rests.

AISLE (Lat. *ala*).—The side subdivision in a church; occasionally all the subdivisions, including the nave, are called aisles.

APSE.—A semicircular or polygonal termination to, or projection from, a church or other public building.

ARCADE.—A range of arches, supported on piers or columns.

ARCH.—A construction of wedge-shaped blocks of stone, or of bricks, of a curved outline, and spanning an open space. The principal forms of arch in use are Semicircular; Acutely-pointed, or Lancet; Equilateral, or Less Acutely-pointed; Four-centred, or Depressed Tudor; Three-centred, or Elliptic; Ogival; Segmental; and Stilted. (Figs. *a* to *f*.)

ARCHITRAVE.—(1) The stone which in Classic and Renaissance architecture is thrown from one column or pilaster to the next. (2) The moulding which in the same styles is used to ornament the margin of a door or window opening or arch.

ASHLAR.—Finely-wrought masonry, employed for the facing of a wall of coarser masonry or brick.

ATTIC (In Renaissance Architecture).—A low upper story, distinctly marked in the architecture of the building, usually surmounting an order; (2) in ordinary building, any story in a roof.

BAILEY (from *vallum*).—The enclosure of the courtyard of a castle.

BALL-FLOWER.—An ornament representing a globular bud, placed usually in a hollow moulding.

BALUSTER.—A species of small column, generally of curved outline.

BALUSTRADE.—A parapet or rail formed of balusters.

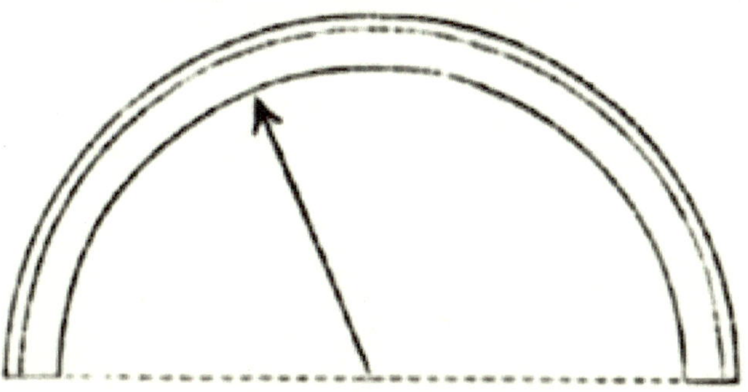

FIG. A.—SEMICIRCULAR ARCH.

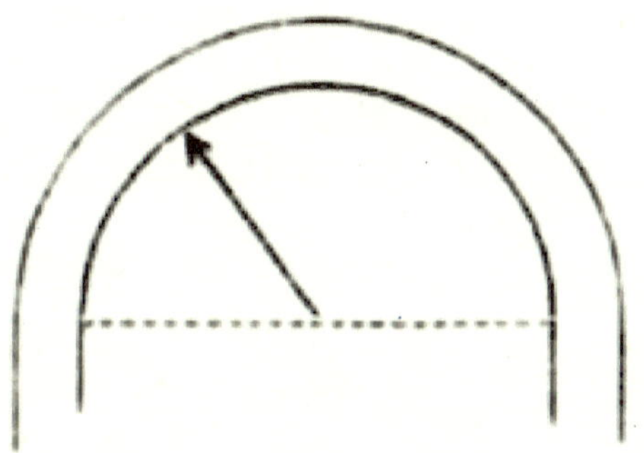

FIG. B.—STILTED ARCH.

The Semicircular and the Stilted Semicircular Arch were the only arches in use till the introduction of the Pointed Arch. Throughout the Early English, Decorated, and Perpendicular periods they occur as exceptional features, but they were practically superseded after the close of the 12th cent.

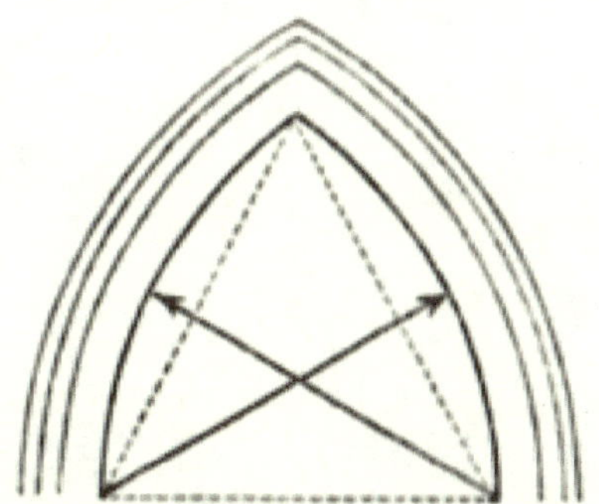

FIG. C.—EQUILATERAL ARCH.

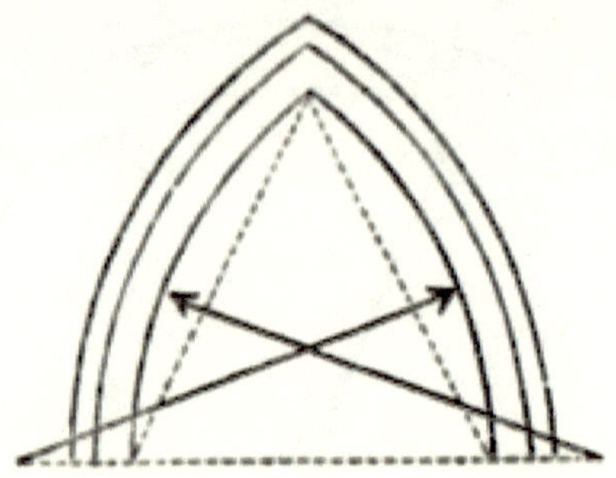

FIG. D.—LANCET ARCH.

The Lancet Arch was characteristic of the Early English period, is never found earlier, and but rarely occurs later. The Equilateral Arch was the favourite arch of the architects of the geometrical Decorated, but is not unfrequently met with in the early part of the Perpendicular period.

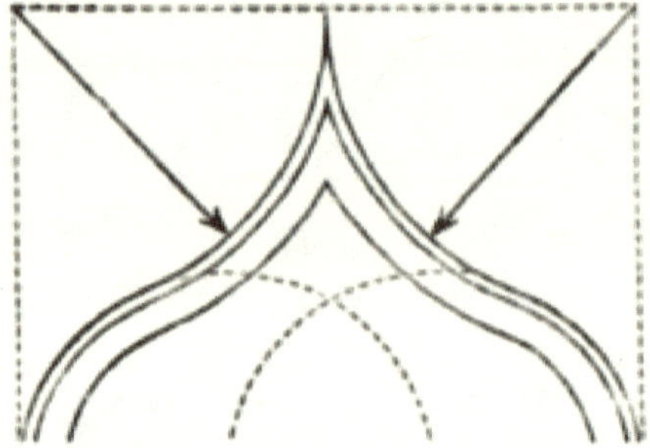

FIG. E.—OGIVAL ARCH.

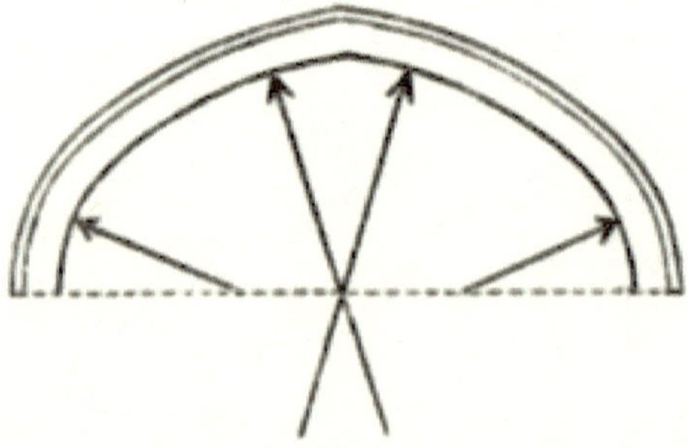

FIG. F.—DEPRESSED TUDOR ARCH.

The Depressed (or Four-centred) Tudor Arch is characteristic of the Perpendicular period, and was then constantly employed. The Ogival Arch is occasionally employed late in that period, but was more used by French and Italian architects than by those of Great Britain.

BAND.—A flat moulding or projecting strip of stone.

BARREL-VAULTING. —See Waggon-head vaulting.

BARGE-BOARD (OR VERGE-BOARD). —An inclined and pierced or ornamented board placed along the edge of a roof when it overhangs a gable wall.

BASE. —(1) The foot of a column; (2) sometimes that of a buttress or wall.

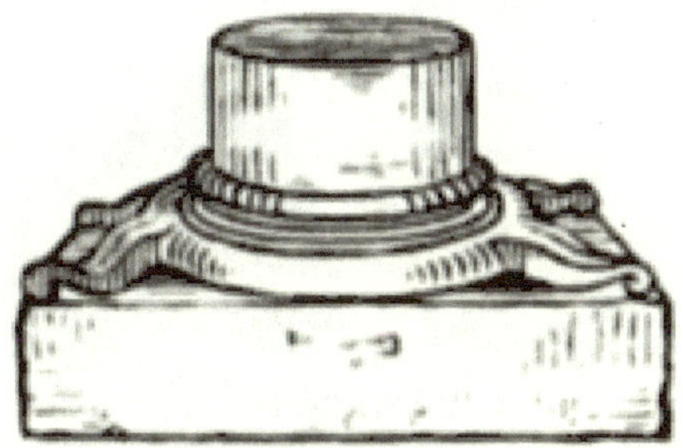

FIG. G.—BASE OF EARLY ENGLISH SHAFT.

FIG. H.—BASE OF PERPENDICULAR SHAFT.

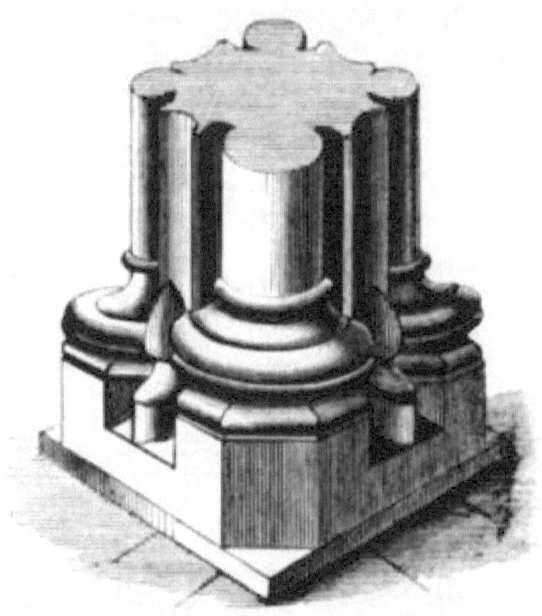

FIG. I.—BASE OF DECORATED SHAFT.

BASILICA.—(1) A Roman public hall; (2) an early Christian church, similar to a Roman basilica in disposition.

BASTION (in Fortification).—A bold projecting mass of building, or earthwork thrown out beyond the general line of a wall.

BATTLEMENT.—A notched or indented parapet.

BAY.—One of the compartments in a building which is made up of several repetitions of the same group of features; *e.g.*, in a church the space from one column of the nave arcade to the next is a bay.

BAY-WINDOW.—A window projecting outward from the wall. It may be rectangular or polygonal. It must be built up from the ground. If thrown out above the ground level, a projecting window is called an Oriel. (See Bow window.)

BEAD.—A small moulding of circular profile.

BELFRY.—A chamber fitted to receive a peal of bells.

BELFRY STAGE.—The story of a tower where the belfry occurs. Usually marked by large open arches or windows, to let the sound escape.

BELL (of a capital).—The body between the necking and the abacus (which see).

BILLET MOULDING.—A moulding consisting of a group of small blocks separated by spaces about equal to their own length.

BLIND STORY.—Triforium (which see).

Boss.—A projecting mass of carving placed to conceal the intersection of the ribs of a vault, or at the end of a string course which it is desired to stop, or in an analogous situation.

Bow Window.—Similar to a Bay-window (which see), but circular or segmental.

Broach-spire.—A spire springing from a tower without a parapet and with pyramidal features at the feet of its four oblique sides (see Fig. 22) to connect them to the four angles of the tower.

Broachead (Spire).—Formed as above described.

Buttress.—A projection built up against a wall to create additional strength or furnish support (see Flying Buttress).

Byzantine.—The round-arched Christian architecture of the Eastern Church, which had its origin in Byzantium (Constantinople).

Canopy.—(1) An ornamented projection over doors, windows, &c.; (2) a covering over niches, tombs, &c.

Campanile.—The Italian name for a bell-tower.

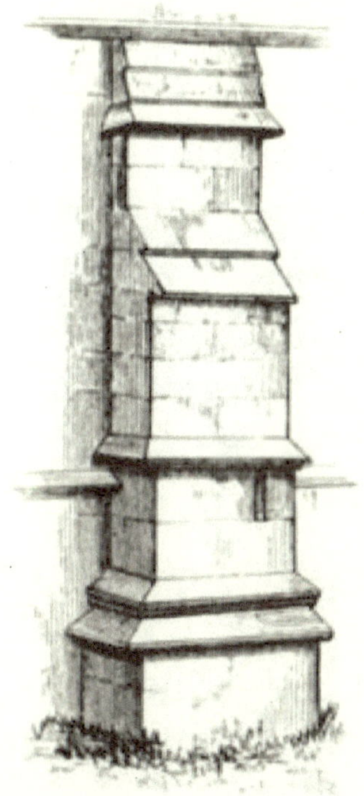

FIG. J.—BUTTRESS.

Capital.—The head of a column or pilaster (Figs. *l* to *p*).

Cathedral.—A church which contains the seat of a bishop; usually a building of the first class.

CERTOSA.—A monastery (or church) of Carthusian monks.

CHAMFER.—A slight strip pared off from a sharp angle.

CHANCEL.—The choir or eastern part of a church.

CHANTRY CHAPEL.—A chapel connected with a monument or tomb in which masses were to be chanted. This was usually of small size and very rich.

CHAPEL.—(1) A chamber attached to a church and opening out of it, or formed within it, and in which an altar was placed; (2) a small detached church.

CHAPTER HOUSE.—The hall of assembly of the chapter (dean and canons) of a cathedral.

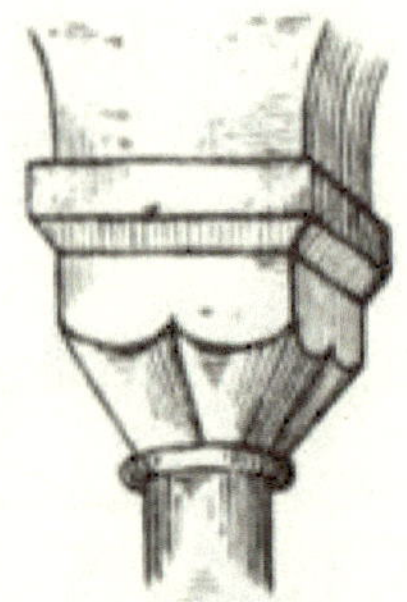

FIG. L.—EARLY NORMAN CAPITAL.

FIG. M.—EARLY ENGLISH CAPITAL.

FIG. N.—LATER NORMAN CAPITAL.

FIG. O.—PERPENDICULAR CAPITAL.

FIG. P.—EARLY FRENCH CAPITAL.

CHÂTEAU.—The French name for a country mansion.

CHEVRON.—A zig-zag ornament.

CHEVET.—The French name for an apse when surrounded by chapels; see the plan of Westminster Abbey (Fig. 6).

CHOIR.—The part of a church in which the services are celebrated; usually, but not always, the east end or chancel. In a Spanish church the choir is often at the crossing.

CLERESTORY.—The upper story or row of windows lighting the nave of a Gothic church.

CLOISTER.—A covered way round a quadrangle of a monastic building.

CLUSTERED (SHAFTS).—Grouped so as to form a pier of some mass out of several small shafts.

CORBEL.—A projecting stone (or timber) supporting, or seeming to support, a weight (Fig. *k*).

FIG. K.—EARLY RENAISSANCE CORBEL.

Corbelling.—A series of mouldings doing the same duty as a corbel; a row of corbels.

Corbel Table.—A row of corbels supporting an overhanging parapet or cornice.

Cortile (Italian).—The internal arcaded quadrangle of a palace, mansion, or public building.

Column.—A stone or marble post, divided usually into base, shaft, and capital; distinguished from a pier by the shaft being cylindrical or polygonal, and in one, or at most, in few pieces.

Cornice.—The projecting and crowning portion of an order (which see) or of a building, or of a stage or story of a building.

Course.—A horizontal layer of stones in the masonry of a building.

Crocket.—A tuft of leaves arranged in a formal shape, used to decorate ornamental gables, the ribs of spires, &c.

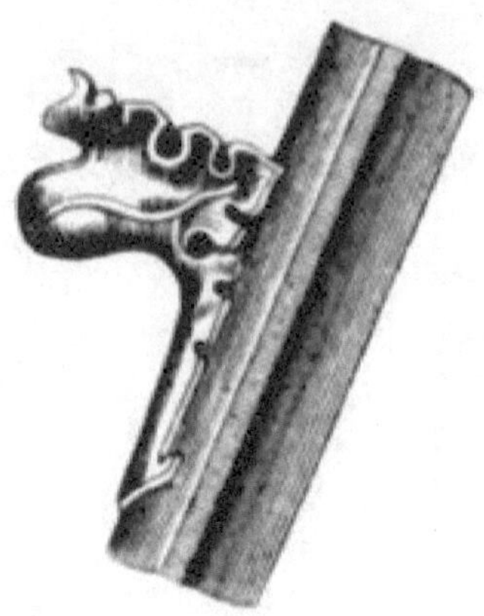

FIG. Q.—DECORATED CROCKET.

FIG. R.—PERPENDICULAR CROCKET.

CROSSING.—The intersection (which see) in a church or cathedral.

CROSS VAULT.—A vault of which the arched surfaces intersect one another, forming a groin (which see).

CRYPT.—The basement under a church or other building (almost invariably vaulted).

CUSP.—The projecting point thrown out to form the leaf-shaped forms or foliations in the heads of Gothic windows, and in tracery and panels.

Dec.   } The Gothic architecture of the fourteenth century in
Decorated.   } England. *Abbreviated* Dec.

DETAIL.—The minuter features of a design or building, especially its mouldings and carving.

DIAPER (Gothic).—An uniform pattern of leaves or flowers carved or painted on the surface of a wall.

FIG. S.—DIAPER IN SPANDREL, FROM WESTMINSTER ABBEY.

DOGTOOTH.—A sharply-pointed ornament in a hollow moulding which is peculiar to Early English Gothic. It somewhat resembles a blunt tooth.

DORMER WINDOW.—A window pierced through a sloping roof and placed under a small gable or roof of its own.

DOME.—A cupola or spherical convex roof, ordinarily circular on plan.

DOMICAL VAULTING.—Vaulting in which a series of small domes are employed; in contradistinction to a waggon-head vault, or an intersecting vault.

DOUBLE TRACERY.—Two layers of tracery one behind the other and with a clear space between.

E. E. Early English.	} The Gothic architecture of England in the thirteenth century. *Abbreviated* E. E.

EAVES.—The verge or edge of a roof overhanging the wall.

EAVES-COURSE.—A moulding carrying the eaves.

ELEVATION.—(1) A geometrical drawing of part of the exterior or interior walls of a building; (2) the architectural treatment of the exterior or interior walls of a building.

Elizabethan.—The architecture of England in, and for some time after, the reign of Elizabeth.

Embattled.—Finished with battlements, or in imitation of battlements.

Enrichments.—The carved (or coloured) decorations applied to the mouldings or other features of an architectural design. (See Mouldings.)

Entablature (in Classic and Renaissance architecture).—The superstructure above the columns where an order is employed. It is divided into the architrave, which rests on the columns, the frieze and the cornice.

Façade.—The front of a building or of a principal part of a building.

Fan Vault.—The vaulting in use in England in the fifteenth century, in which a series of conoids bearing some resemblance to an open fan are employed.

Fillet.—A small moulding of square flat section.

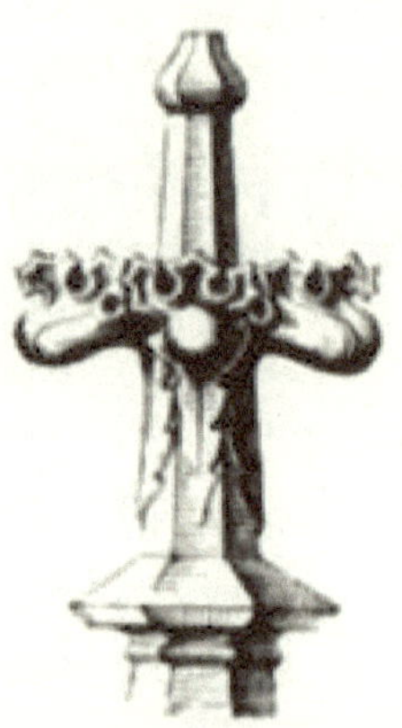

FIG. T.—PERPENDICULAR FINIAL.

Finial.—A formally arranged bunch of foliage or other similar ornament forming the top of a pinnacle, gablet, or other ornamented feature of Gothic architecture.

Flamboyant Style.—The late Gothic architecture of France at the end of the fifteenth century, so called from the occurrence of flame-shaped forms in the tracery.

Flèche.—A name adapted from the French. A slender spire, mostly placed on a roof; not often so called if on a tower.

Flying Buttress.—A buttress used to steady the upper and inner walls of a vaulted building, placed at some distance from the wall which it supports, and connected with it by an arch.

FIG. U.—FLYING BUTTRESS.

Foil.—A leaf-shaped form produced by adding cusps to the curved outline of a window head or piece of tracery.

Foliation.—The decoration of an opening, or of tracery by means of foils and cusps.

Fosse.—The ditch of a fortress.

François I. Style.—The early Renaissance architecture of France during part of the sixteenth century.

Frieze.—(1) The middle member of a Classic or Renaissance entablature; this was often sculptured and carved; (2) any band of sculptured ornament.

Gable.—The triangular-shaped wall carrying the end of a roof.

Gablet.—A small gable (usually ornamental only).

Gallery.—(1) An apartment of great length in proportion to its width; (2) a raised floor or stage in a building.

Gargoyle.—A projecting waterspout, usually carved in stone, more rarely formed of metal.

GEOMETRICAL.—The architecture of the earlier part of the decorated period in England.

GRILLE.—A grating or ornamental railing of metal.

GROIN.—The curved line which is made by the meeting of the surfaces of two vaults or portions of vaults which intersect.

GROUP.—An assemblage of shafts or mouldings or other small features intended to produce a combined effect.

GROUPING.—Combining architectural features as above.

HALL.—(1) The largest room in an ancient English mansion, or a college, &c.; (2) any large and stately apartment.

HALF TIMBERED CONSTRUCTION.—A mode of building in which a framework of timbers is displayed and the spaces between them are filled in with plaster or tiles.

HAMMER BEAM ROOF.—A roof peculiar to English architecture of the fifteenth century, deriving its name from the use of a hammer beam (a large bracket projecting from the walls) to partly support the rafters.

HEAD (of an arch or other opening).—The portion within the curve; whether filled in by masonry or left open, sometimes called a tympanum.

HIP.—The external angle formed by the meeting of two sloping sides of a roof where there is no gable.

HÔTEL (French).—A town mansion.

IMPOST.—A moulding or other line marking the top of the jambs of an arched opening, and the starting point, or apparent starting point, of the arch.

INLAY.—A mode of decoration in which coloured materials are laid into sinkings of ornamental shape, cut into the surface to be decorated.

INTERSECTION (OR CROSSING).—The point in a church where the transepts cross the nave.

INTERSECTING VAULTS.—Vaults of which the surfaces cut one another.

INTERPENETRATION.—A German mode of treating mouldings, as though two or more sets of them existed in the same stone and they could pass through (interpenetrate) each other.

JAMB.—The side of a door or window or arch, or other opening.

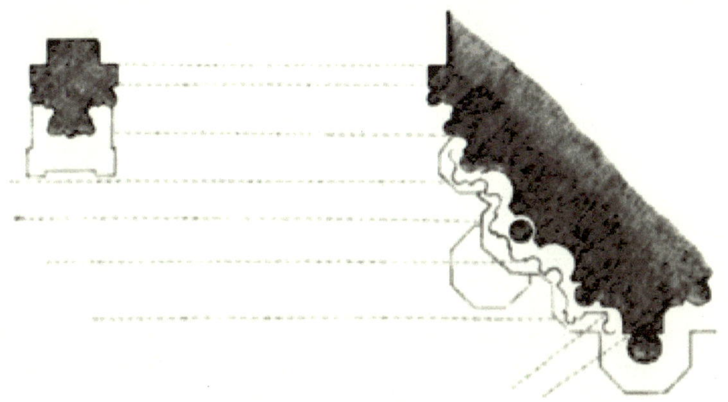

FIG. V.—PLAN OF A JAMB AND CENTRAL PIER OF A GOTHIC DOORWAY.

KEEP.—The tower which formed the stronghold of a mediæval castle.

KING POST.—The middle post in the framing of a timber roof.

LANCET ARCH.—The sharply-pointed window-head and arch, characteristic of English Gothic in the thirteenth century.

LANTERN.—A conspicuous feature rising above a roof or crowning a dome, and intended usually to light a Hall, but often introduced simply as an architectural finish to the whole building.

LIERNE (rib).—A rib intermediate between the main ribs in Gothic vaulting.

LIGHT.—One of the divisions of a window of which the entire width is divided by one or more mullions.

LINTEL.—The stone or beam covering a doorway or other opening not spanned by an arch. Sometimes applied to the architrave of an order.

LOGGIA (Italian).—An open arcade with a gallery behind.

LOOP.—Short for loophole. A very narrow slit in the wall of a fortress, serving as a window, or to shoot through.

LUCARNE.—A spire-light. A small window like a slender dormer window.

MOAT (or Fosse).—The ditch round a fortress or semi-fortified house.

MOSAIC.—An ornament for pavements, walls, and the surfaces of vaults, formed by cementing together small pieces of coloured material (stone, marble, tile, &c.) so as to produce a pattern or picture.

MOULDING.—A term applied to all varieties of contour or outline given to the angles, projections, or recesses of the various parts of a building. The object being either to produce an outline satisfactory to the eye; or, more frequently, to obtain a play of light and shade, and to produce the appearance of a line or a series of lines, broad or narrow, and of varying intensity of lightness or shade in the building or some of its features.

The contour which a moulding would present when cut across in a direction at right angles to its length is called its profile.

The profile of mouldings varied with each style of architecture and at each period (Figs. *w* to *z*). When ornaments are carved out of some of the moulded surfaces the latter are technically termed enriched mouldings. The enrichments in use varied with each style and each period, as the mouldings themselves did.

MULLION.—The upright bars of stone frequently employed (especially in Gothic architecture) to subdivide one window into two or more lights.

NAVE.—(1) The central avenue of a church or cathedral; (2) the western part of a church as distinguished from the chancel or choir; (3) occasionally, any avenue in the interior of a building which is divided by one or more rows of columns running lengthways is called a nave.

NECKING (of a column).—The point (usually marked by a fillet or other small projecting moulding) where the shaft ends and the capital begins.

NEWEL POST.—The stout post at the foot of a staircase from which the balustrade or the handrail starts.

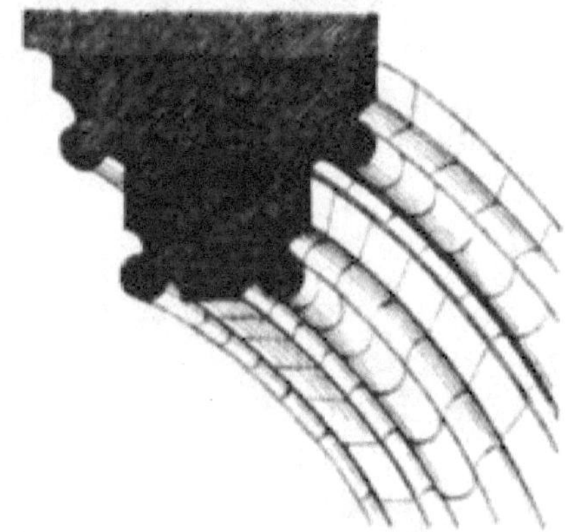

FIG. W.—ARCH MOULDING. (GOTHIC, 12TH CENTURY.)

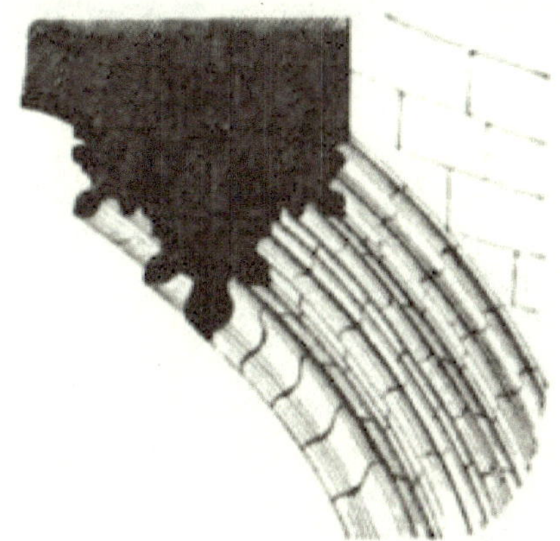

FIG. Y.—ARCH MOULDING. (DECORATED, 14TH CENTURY.)

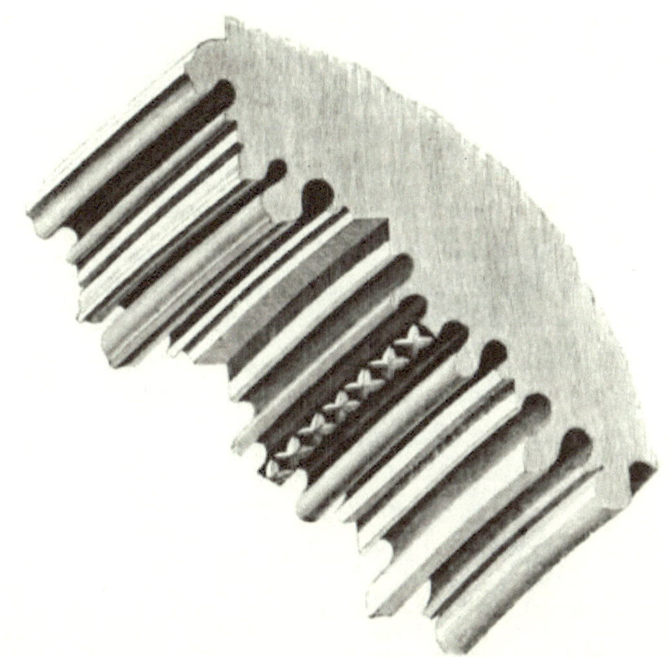

FIG. Z.—ARCH MOULDING. (GOTHIC, 13TH CENTURY.)

NICHE.—A recess in a wall for a statue, vase, or other upright ornament.

NORMAN.—The architecture of England from the Norman Conquest till the latter part of the twelfth century.

OGEE.—A moulding or line of part concave and part convex curvature (see Fig. *e*, showing an ogee-shaped arch).

OGIVAL.—Ogee-shaped (see Fig. 54).

Open Tracery.—Tracery in which the spaces between the bars are neither closed by slabs of stone nor glazed.

Order.—(1) In Classical and Renaissance architecture a single column or pilaster and its appropriate entablature or superstructure; (2) a series of columns or pilasters with their entablature; (3) an entire decorative system appropriate to the kind of column chosen. In Renaissance architecture there are five orders—the Tuscan, Doric, Ionic, Corinthian, and Composite. Each has its own proper column, and its proper base, shaft, and capital; and its own entablature. The proportions and the degree of enrichment appropriate to each vary. The Tuscan being the sturdiest and plainest, the Composite the most slender and most small, and the others taking place in the succession in which they stand enumerated above. Where more than one order occurs in a building, as constantly happens in Classic and Renaissance buildings, the orders which are the plainest and most sturdy (and have been named first) if employed, are invariably placed below the more slender orders; *e.g.* the Doric is never placed *over* the Corinthian or the Ionic, but if employed in combination with either of those orders it is always the lowest in position.

Oriel.—A window projecting like a bay or bow window, not resting on the ground but thrown out above the ground level and resting on a corbel.

Palladian.—A phase of fully developed Renaissance architecture introduced by the architect Palladio, and largely followed in England as well as in Italy.

Panel.—(1) The thinner portions of the framed woodwork of doors and other such joiner's work; (2) all sunk compartments in masonry, ceilings, &c.

Panelling.—(1) Woodwork formed of framework containing panels; (2) any decoration formed of a series of sunk compartments.

Parapet.—A breastwork or low wall used to protect the gutters and screen the roofs of buildings; also, perhaps primarily, to protect the ramparts of fortifications.

FIG. A A.—OPEN PARAPET, LATE DECORATED.

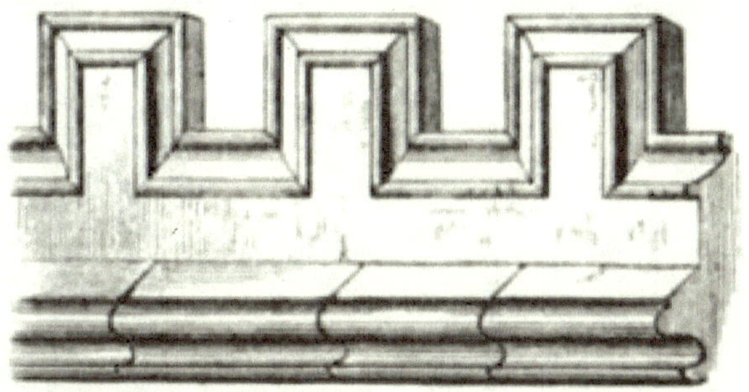

FIG. B B.—BATTLEMENTED PARAPET, PERPENDICULAR.

PAVILION.—A strongly marked single block of building; most frequently applied to those blocks in French and other Renaissance buildings that are marked out by high roofs.

PEDESTAL.—(1) A substructure sometimes placed under a column in Renaissance architecture; (2) a similar substructure intended to carry a statue, vase, or other ornament.

PEDIMENT.—(1) The gable, where used in Renaissance buildings; (2) an ornamental gable sometimes placed over windows, doors, and other features in Gothic buildings.

Perp.
Perpendicular.   } The Gothic architecture of the fifteenth century in England. *Abbreviated* Perp.

PIER.—(1) A mass of walling, either a detached portion of a wall or a distinct structure of masonry, taking the place of a column in the arcade of a church or elsewhere; (2) a group or cluster of shafts substituted for a column.

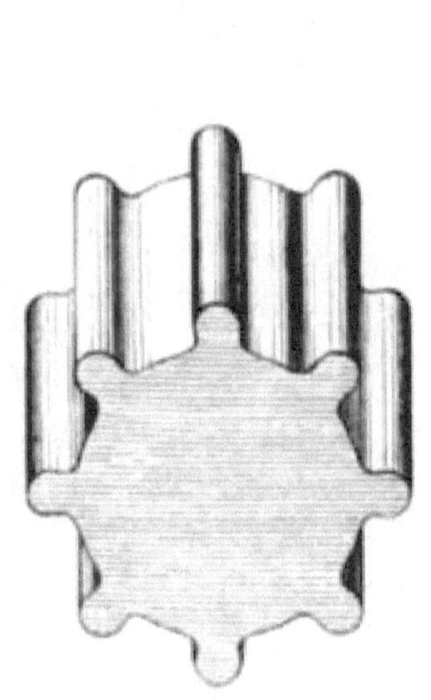

FIG. C C.—EARLY ENGLISH PIERS.

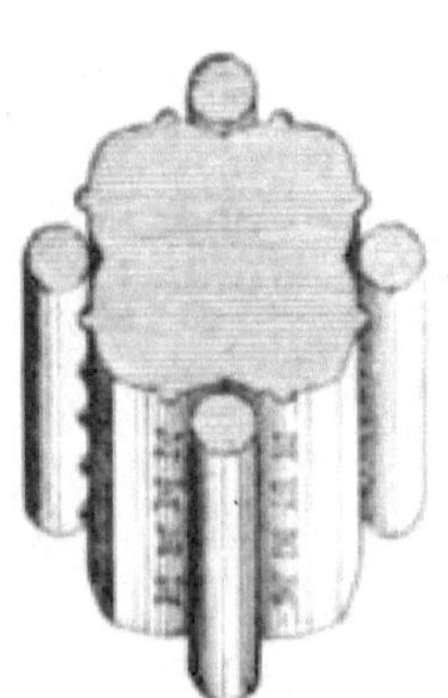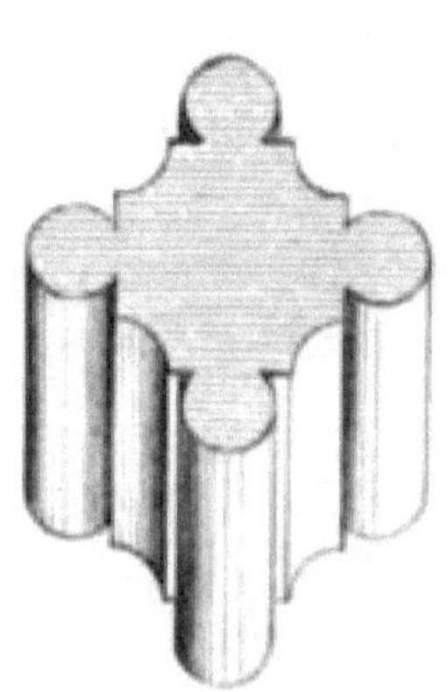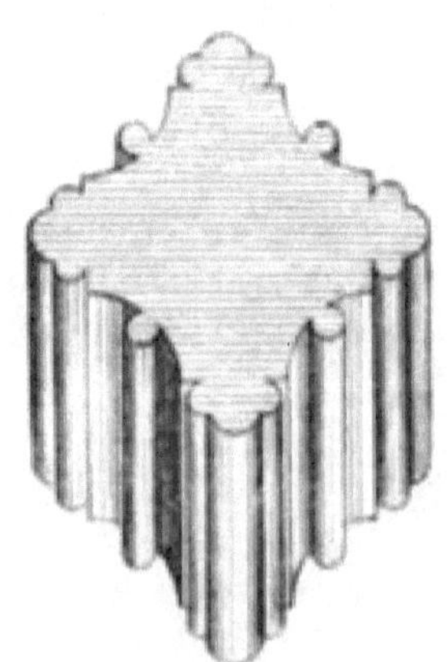

FIG. D D.—LATE DECORATED AND PERPENDICULAR PIERS.

PILASTER.—A square column, usually attached to a wall; frequently used in Classic and Renaissance architecture in combination with columns.

PINNACLE (in Gothic architecture).—A small turret, or ornament, usually with a pointed top, employed to mark the summit of gables, buttresses, and other tall features.

PITCH.—The degree of slope given to a roof, gable, or pediment.

PLAN.—(1) A map of the floor of a building, showing the piers, if any, and the walls which inclose and divide it, with the openings in them; (2) the actual arrangement and disposition of the floors, piers, and walls of the building itself.

PLANE.—The imaginary surface within which a series of mouldings lies, and which coincides with the salient and important points of that series. Mouldings are said to be on an oblique plane when their plane forms an angle less than a right angle with the face of the wall; and in receding planes, when they can be divided into a series of groups of more or less stepped outline, each within and behind the other, and each partly bounded by a plane parallel with the face of the wall.

PLASTER.—The plastic material, of which the groundwork is lime and sand, used to cover walls internally and to form ceilings. Sometimes employed as a covering to walls externally.

PLINTH.—The base of a wall or of a column or range of columns.

PORTAL.—A dignified and important entrance doorway.

PORTICO.—A range of columns with their entablature (and usually covered by a pediment), marking the entrance to a Renaissance or Classic building.

PRISMATIC RUSTICATION.—In Elizabethan architecture rusticated masonry with diamond-shaped projections worked on the face of each stone.

PROFILE.—The contour or outline of mouldings as they would appear if sawn across at right angles to their length.

PORCH.—A small external structure to protect and ornament the doorway to a building (rarely met with in Renaissance).

QUATREFOIL.—A four-leaved ornament occupying a circle in tracery or a panel.

RAFTERS.—The sloping beams of a roof upon which the covering of the roof rests.

RAGSTONE.—A coarse stone found in parts of Kent and elsewhere, and used for walling.

RECEDING PLANES.—(See Plane.)

RECESS.—A sinking in a building deeper than a mere panel.

RECESSING.—Forming one or more recesses. Throwing back some part of a building behind the general face.

RENAISSANCE.—The art of the period of the Classic revival which began in the sixteenth century. In this volume used chiefly to denote the architecture of Europe in that and the succeeding centuries.

RIB (in Gothic vaulting).—A bar of masonry or moulding projecting beyond the general surface of a vault, to mark its intersections or subdivide its surface, and to add strength.

RIDGE.—(1) The straight line or ornament which marks the summit of a roof; (2) the line or rib, straight or curved, which marks the summit of a vault.

ROLL.—A round moulding.

ROSE WINDOW.—A wheel window (which see).

RUBBLE.—Rough stonework forming the heart of a masonry wall; sometimes faced with ashlar (which see), sometimes shown.

RUSTICATION (or RUSTICATED MASONRY).—The sort of ornamental ashlar masonry (chiefly Classic and Renaissance) in which each stone is distinguished by a broad channel all round it, marking the joints.

RUSTICS.—The individual blocks of stone used in rustication (as described above).

SCREEN.—An internal partition or inclosure cutting off part of a building. At the entrance to the choir of a church screens of beautiful workmanship were used.

SCROLL MOULDING.—A round roll moulding showing a line along its face (distinctive of decorated Gothic).

SCROLL WORK.—Ornament showing winding spiral lines like the edge of a scroll of paper (chiefly found in Elizabethan).

SECTION.—(1) A drawing of a building as it would appear if cut through at some fixed plane. (2) That part of the construction of a building which would be displayed by such a drawing as described above. (3) The profile of a moulding.

SET-OFF.—A small ledge formed by diminishing the thickness of a wall or pier.

SEXPARTITE VAULTING.—Where each bay or compartment is divided by its main ribs into six portions.

SGRAFFITO (Italian).—An ornament produced by scratching lines on the plastered face of a building so as to show a different colour filling up the lines or surfaces scratched away.

SHAFT.—(1) The middle part of a column between its base and capital. (2) In Gothic, slender columns introduced for ornamental purposes, singly or in clusters.

SHELL ORNAMENT.—A decoration frequently employed in Italian and French Renaissance, and resembling the interior of a shell.

SKY-LINE.—The outline which a building will show against the sky.

SPANDREL.—The triangular (or other shaped) space between the outside of an arch and the mouldings, or surfaces inclosing it or in contact with it. (See Fig. *s*, under Diaper.)

SPIRE.—The steep and pointed roof of a tower (usually a church tower).

SPIRE-LIGHT (or LUCARNE).—A dormer window (which see) in a spire.

SPLAY.—A slope making with the face of a wall an angle less than a right angle.

STAGE.—One division in the height of any building or portion of a building where horizontal divisions are distinctly marked, *e.g.*, the belfry stage of a tower, the division in which the bells are hung.

STEEPLE.—A tower and spire in combination. Sometimes applied to a tower or spire separately.

STEPPED GABLE.—A gable in which, instead of a sloping line, the outline is formed by a series of steps.

STILTED ARCH.—An arch of which the curve does not commence till above the level of the impost (which see).

STORY.—(1) The portion of a building between one floor and the next; (2) any stage or decidedly marked horizontal compartment of a building, even if not corresponding to an actual story marked by a floor.

STRAP-WORK (Elizabethan).—An ornament representing strap-like fillets interlaced.

STRING-COURSE.—A projecting horizontal (or occasionally sloping) band or line of mouldings.

TABERNACLE WORK.—The richly ornamented and carved work with which the smaller and more precious features of a church, *e.g.*, the fittings of a choir, were adorned and made conspicuous.

TERMINAL (or Finial).—The ornamental top of a pinnacle, gable, &c.

TERRA-COTTA.—A fine kind of brick capable of being highly ornamented, and formed into blocks of some size.

THRUST.—The pressure exercised laterally by an arch or vault, or by the timbers of a roof on the abutments or supports.

TIE.—A beam of wood, bar of iron, or similar expedient employed to hold together the feet or sides of an arch, vault, or roof, and so counteract the thrust.

TORUS.—A large convex moulding.

TOWER.—A portion of a building rising conspicuously above the general mass, and obviously distinguished by its height from that mass. A detached building of which the height is great, relative to the width and breadth.

TRACERY (Gothic).—The ornamental stonework formed by the curving and interlacing of bars of stone, and occupying the heads of windows, panels, and other situations where decoration and lightness have to be combined. The simplest and earliest tracery might be described as a combination of openings pierced through the stone head of an arch. Cusping and foliation (which see) are features of tracery. (See Figs. 18, 19, 55, and 57 in the text.)

FIG. E E.—PERPENDICULAR WINDOW-HEAD.

FIG. F F.—LATE PERPENDICULAR WINDOW-HEAD.

TRANSEPT.—The arms of a church or cathedral which cross the line of the nave.

TRANSITION.—The architecture of a period coming between and sharing the characteristics of two distinctly marked styles or phases of architecture, one of which succeeded the other.

TRANSOM.—A horizontal bar (usually of stone) across a window or panel.

TREFOIL.—A three-leaved or three-lobed form found constantly in the heads of windows and in other situations where tracery is employed.

TRIFORIUM (or THOROUGH-FARE).—The story in a large church or cathedral intermediate between the arcade separating the nave and aisles, and the clerestory.

TUDOR.—The architecture of England during the reigns of the Tudor kings. The use of the term is usually, however, restricted to a period which closes with the end of Henry VIII.'s reign, 1547.

TURRET.—A small tower, sometimes rising from the ground, but often carried on corbels and commencing near the upper part of the building to which it is an appendage.

TYMPANUM.—The filling in of the head of an arch, or occasionally of an ornamental gable.

UNDERCUTTING.—A moulding or ornament of which the greater part stands out from the mouldings or surfaces which it adjoins, as though almost or quite detached from them, is said to be undercut.

VAULT.—An arched ceiling to a building, or part of a building, executed in masonry or in some substitute for masonry.

The vaults of the Norman period were simple barrel- or waggon-headed vaults, and semicircular arches only were used in their construction. With the Gothic period the use of intersecting, and as a result of pointed arches, was introduced into vaulting, and vaults went on increasing in complexity and elaboration till the Tudor period, when fan-vaulting was employed. Our illustrations show some of the steps in the development of Gothic vaults referred to in Chapter V. of the text. No. 1 represents a waggon-head vault with an intersecting vault occupying part of its length. No. 2 represents one of the expedients adopted for vaulting an oblong compartment before the pointed arch was introduced. The narrower arch is stilted and the line of the groin is not true. No. 3 represents a similar compartment vaulted without any distortion or irregularity by the help of the pointed arch. No. 4 represents one lay of a sexpartite Gothic vault. No. 5 represents a vault with lierne ribs making a star-shaped pallom on plan, and No. 6 is a somewhat more intricate example of the same class of vault.

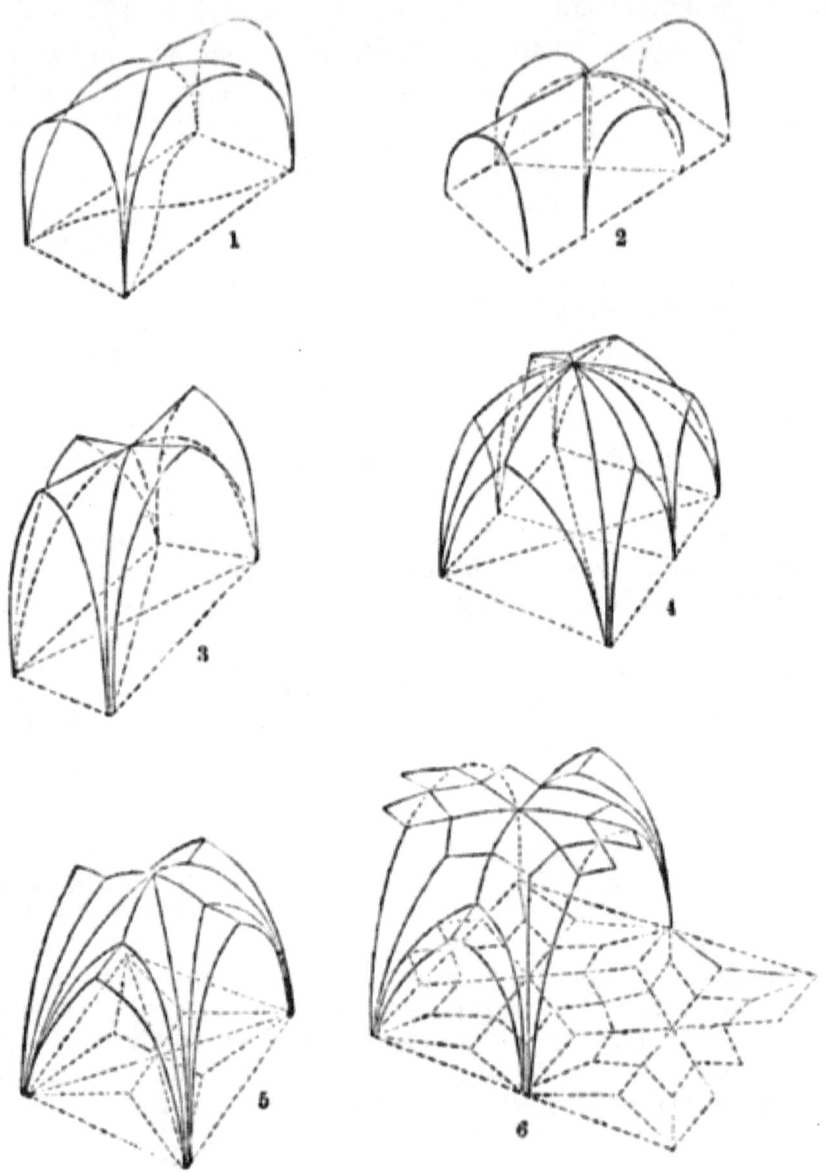

FIG. G G.—VAULTS.

Vaults are met with in Renaissance buildings, but they are a less distinctive feature of such buildings than they were in the Gothic period; and in many cases where a vault or a series of vaults would have been employed by a Gothic architect, a Renaissance architect has preferred to make use of a dome or a series of domes. This is called domical vaulting. Examples of it occur occasionally in Gothic work.

WAGGON-HEAD VAULTING, OR BARREL-VAULTING. — A simple form of tunnel-like vaulting, which gets its name from its resemblance to the tilt often seen over large waggons, or to the half of a barrel.

WAINSCOT. — (1) The panelling often employed to line the walls of a room or building; (2) a finely marked variety of oak imported chiefly from Holland; probably so called because wainscot oak was at one time largely employed for such panelling.

WEATHERING. — A sloping surface of stone employed to cover the set-off (which see) of a wall or buttress and protect it from the effects of weather.

WHEEL WINDOW. — A circular window, and usually one in which mullions radiate from a centre towards the circumference like the spokes of a wheel; sometimes called a rose-window.

WINDOW-HEAD. — For illustrations of the various forms and filling-in of Gothic window-heads, see the words Arch and Tracery.

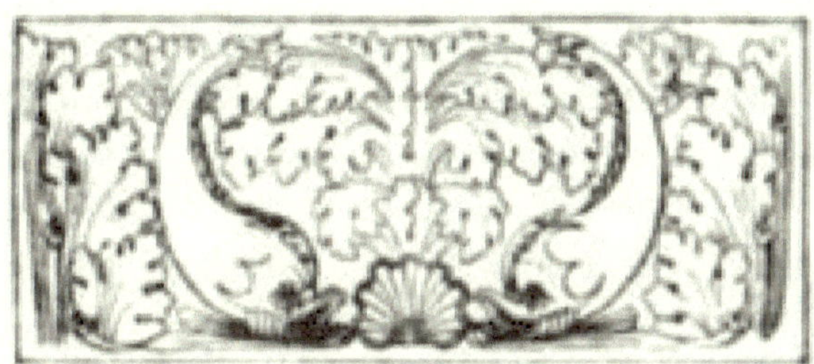

HEAD AND TAILPIECES.

The End-papers are from a Tapestry in Hardwick Hall.

THE LILY OF FLORENCE.

GOTHIC ARCHITECTURE.

CHAPTER I.

INTRODUCTION.

THE architecture generally known as Gothic, but often described as Christian Pointed, prevailed throughout Europe to the exclusion of every rival for upwards of three centuries; and it is to be met with, more or less, during two others. Speaking broadly, it may be said that its origin took place in the twelfth century, that the thirteenth was the period of its development, the fourteenth that of its perfection, and the fifteenth that of its decline; while many examples of its employment occur in the sixteenth.

In the following chapters the principal changes in the features of buildings which occurred during the progress of the style in England will be described. Subsequently, the manner in which the different stages of development were reached in different countries will be given; for architecture passed through very nearly the same phases in all European nations, though not quite simultaneously.

It must be understood that through the whole Gothic period, growth or at least change was going on; the transitions from one stage to another were only periods of more rapid change than usual. The whole process may be illustrated by the progress of a language. If, for instance, we compare round-arched architecture in the eleventh century to the Anglo-Saxon form of speech of the time of Alfred the Great, and the architecture of the twelfth century to the English of Chaucer, that of the thirteenth will correspond to the richer language of Shakespeare, that of the fourteenth to the highly polished language of Addison and Pope, and that of the fifteenth to the English of our own day. We can thus obtain an apt parallel to the gradual change and growth which went on in architecture; and we shall find that the oneness of the language in the former case, and of the architecture in the latter, was maintained throughout.

For an account of the Christian round-arched architecture which preceded Gothic, the reader is referred to the companion volume in this series. Here it will be only necessary briefly to review the circumstances which went before the appearance of the pointed styles.

The Roman empire had introduced into Europe some thing like a universal architecture, so that the buildings of any Roman colony bore a strong resemblance to those of every other colony and of the metropolis; varying, of course, in extent and magnificence, but not much in design. The architecture of the Dark Ages in Western Europe exhibited, so far as is known, the same general similarity. Down to the eleventh century the buildings erected (almost exclusively churches and monastic buildings) were not large or rich, and were heavy in appearance and simple in construction. Their arches were all semicircular.

The first rays of light across the gloom of the Dark Ages seem to have come from the energy and ability of Charlemagne in the eighth century.

In the succeeding century, this activity received a check; an idea became generally prevalent that the year one thousand was to see the end of the world; men's minds were overshadowed with apprehension; and buildings, in common with other undertakings of a permanent nature, were but little attempted.

When the millennium came and passed, and left all as it had been, a kind of revulsion of feeling was experienced; many important undertakings were set on foot, such as during the preceding years it had not been thought worth while to prosecute. The eleventh century thus became a time of great religious activity; and if the First Crusade, which took place 1095, may be taken as one outcome of that pious zeal, another can certainly be found in the large and often costly churches and monasteries which rose in every part of England, France, Germany, Lombardy, and South Italy. Keen rivalry raged among the builders of these churches; each one was built larger and finer than the previous examples, and the details began to grow elaborate. Construction and ornament were in fact advancing and improving, if not from year to year, at any rate from decade to decade, so that by the commencement of the twelfth century a remarkable development had taken place. The ideas of the dimensions of churches then entertained were really almost as liberal as during the best period of Gothic architecture.

An illustration of this fact is furnished by the rebuilding of Westminster Abbey under Edward the Confessor. He pulled down a small church which he found standing on the site, in order to erect one suitable in size and style to the ideas of the day. The style of his cathedral (but not its dimensions) soon became so much out of date that Henry III. pulled the buildings down in order to re-erect them of the lofty proportions and with the pointed arches which we now see in the choir and transepts of the Abbey; but the size remained nearly the same, for there is evidence to show that the Confessor's buildings must have occupied very nearly, if not quite, as much ground as those which succeeded them.

At the beginning of the twelfth century many local peculiarities, some of them due to accident, some to the nature and quality of the building materials obtainable, some to differences of race, climate, and habits, and some to other causes, had begun to make their appearance in the buildings of various parts of Europe; and through the whole Gothic period such peculiarities were to be met with. Still the points of similarity were greater and more numerous than the differences; so much so, that by going through the course which Gothic architecture ran in one of the countries in which it flourished, it will readily be possible to furnish a general outline of the subject as a whole; it will then only be requisite to point out the principal variations in the practice of other countries. On some grounds France would be the most suitable country to select for this purpose, for Gothic appeared earlier and flourished more brilliantly in that country than in any other; the balance of advantage lies however, when writing for English students, in the selection of Great Britain. The various phases through which the art passed are well marked in this country, they have been fully studied and described, and, what is of the greatest importance, English examples are easily accessible to the majority of students, while those which cannot be visited may be very readily studied from engravings and photographs. English Gothic will therefore be first considered; but as a preliminary a few words remain to be said describing generally the buildings which have come down to us from the Gothic period.

The word Gothic, which was in use in the eighteenth century, and probably earlier, was invented at a time when a Goth was synonymous with everything that was barbarous; and its use then implied a reproach. It denotes, according to Mr. Fergusson, "all the styles invented and used by the Western barbarians who overthrew the Roman empire, and settled within its limits."

FIG 1.—WEST ENTRANCE, LICHFIELD CATHEDRAL, (1275.)

(See Chapter V.)

CHAPTER II.
THE BUILDINGS OF THE MIDDLE AGES.

By far the most important specimens of Gothic architecture are the cathedrals and large churches which were built during the prevalence of the style. They were more numerous, larger, and more complete as works of art than any other structures, and accordingly they are to be considered on every account as the best examples of pointed architecture.

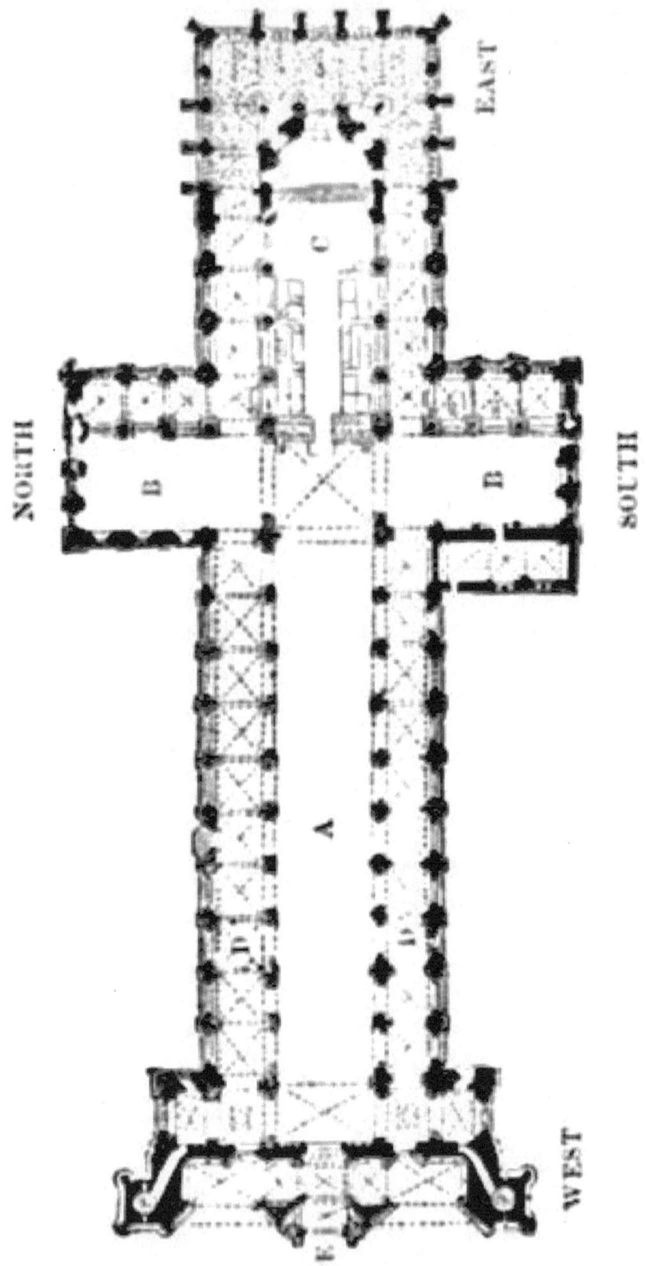

FIG. 2.—GROUND PLAN OF PETERBOROUGH CATHEDRAL. (1118 TO 1193.)

A. Nave. B B. Transepts. C. Choir. D D. Aisles. E. Principal Entrance.

FIG. 3.—TRANSVERSE SECTION OF THE NAVE OF SALISBURY CATHEDRAL.

(A.D. 1217).

The arrangement and construction of a Gothic cathedral were customarily as follows:—(See Fig. 2.) The main axis of the building was always east and west, the principal entrance being at the west end, usually under a grand porch or portal, and the high altar stood at the east end. The plan (or main floor) of the building almost always displays the form of a cross. The stem of the cross is the part from the west entrance to the crossing, and is called the nave. The arms of the cross are called transepts, and point respectively north and south. Their crossing with the nave is often called the intersection. The remaining arm, which prolongs the stem eastwards, is ordinarily called the choir, but sometimes the presbytery, and sometimes the chancel. All these names really refer to the position of the internal fittings of the church, and it is often more accurate simply to employ the term eastern arm for this portion of a church.

The nave is flanked by two avenues running parallel to it, narrower and lower than itself, called aisles. They are separated from it by rows of columns or piers, connected together by arches. Thus the nave has an arcade on each side of it, and each aisle has an arcade on one side, and a main external wall on the other. The aisle walls are usually pierced by windows. The arches of the arcade carry walls which rise above the roofs of the aisles, and light the nave. These walls are usually subdivided internally into two heights or stories; the lower story consists of a series of small arches, to which the name of triforium is given. This arcade usually opens into the dark space above the ceiling or vault of the aisle, and hence it is sometimes called the blind story. The upper story is the range of windows already alluded to as lighting the nave, and is called the clerestory. Thus a spectator standing in the nave, and looking towards the side (Figs. 4 and 5), will see opposite him the main arcade, and over that the triforium, and over that the clerestory, crowned by the nave vault or roof; and looking through the arches of the nave arcade, he will see the side windows of the aisle. Above the clerestory of the nave, and the side windows of the aisles, come the vaults or roofs. In some instances double aisles (two on each side) have been employed.

The transepts usually consist of well-marked limbs, divided like the nave into a centre avenue and two side aisles, and these usually are of the same width and height as the nave and its aisles. Sometimes there are no transepts; sometimes they do not project beyond the line of the walls, but still are marked by their rising above the lower height of the nave aisles. Sometimes the transepts have no aisles, or an aisle only on one side.[1] On the other hand, it is sometimes customary, especially in English examples, to form two pairs of transepts. This occurs in Lichfield Cathedral.

---

[1] As the north transept at Peterborough (Fig. 2).

FIG. 4.—CHOIR OF WORCESTER CATHEDRAL. (BEGUN 1224.)

A. Nave Arcade. B. Triforium. C. Clerestory.

FIG. 5.—NAVE OF WELLS CATHEDRAL. (1206 TO 1242.)

A. Nave Arcade. B. Triforium. C. Clerestory.

The eastern arm of the cathedral is the part to which most importance was attached, and it is usual to mark that importance by greater richness, and by a difference in the height of its roof or vault as compared with the nave; its floor is always raised. It also has its central passage and its aisles; and it has double aisles much more frequently than the nave. The eastern termination of the cathedral is sometimes semicircular, sometimes polygonal, and when it takes this form it is called an apse or an apsidal east end; sometimes it is square, the apse being most in use on the Continent, and the square east end in England. Attached to some of the side walls of the church it is usual to have a series of chapels; these are ordinarily chambers partly shut off from the main structure, but opening into it by arched openings; each chapel contains an altar. The finest chapel is usually one placed on the axis of the cathedral, and east of the east end of the main building; this is called, where it exists, the Lady Chapel, and was customarily dedicated to the Virgin. Henry VII.'s Chapel at Westminster (Fig. 6) furnishes a familiar instance of the lady chapel of a great church. Next in importance rank the side chapels which open out of the aisles of the apse, when there is one. Westminster Abbey furnishes good examples of these also. The eastern wall of the transept is a favourite position for chapels. They are less frequently added to the nave aisles.

The floor of the eastern arm of the cathedral, as has been pointed out, is always raised, so as to be approached by steps; it is inclosed by screen work which shuts off the choir, or inclosure for the performance of divine service, from the nave. The fittings of this part of the building generally include stalls for the clergy and choristers and a bishop's throne, and are usually beautiful works of art. Tombs, and inclosures connected with them, called chantry chapels, are constantly met with in various positions, but most frequently in the eastern arm.

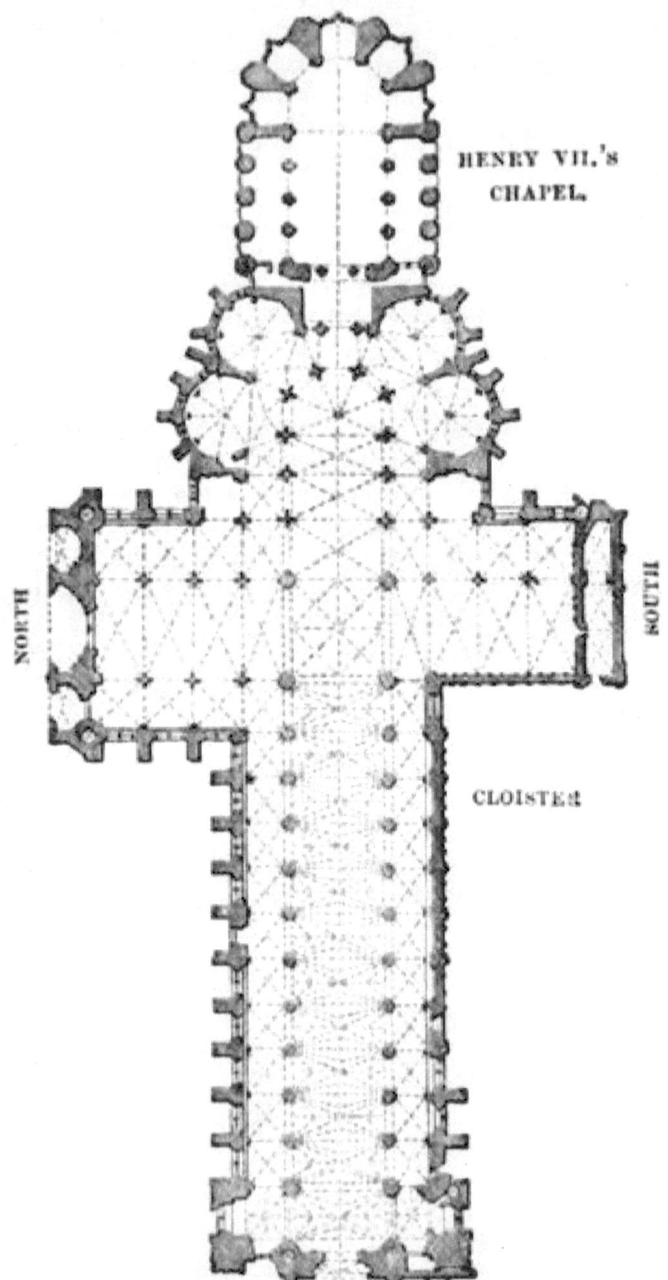

FIG. 6.—GROUND PLAN OF WESTMINSTER ABBEY.

Below the raised floor of the choir, and sometimes below other parts of the building, there often exists a subterranean vaulted structure known as the crypt.

Passing to the exterior of the cathedral, the principal doorway is in the western front:[2] usually supplemented by entrances at the ends of the transepts, and one or more side entrances to the nave. A porch on the north side of the nave is a common feature. The walls are now seen to be strengthened by stone piers, called buttresses. Frequently arches are thrown from these buttresses to the higher walls of the building. The whole arrangement of pier and arch is called a flying buttress,[3] and, as will be explained later, is used to steady the upper part of the building when a stone vault is employed (see Chap. V.). The lofty gables in which the nave and transepts, and the eastern arm when square terminate, form prominent features, and are often occupied by great windows.

In a complete cathedral, the effect of the exterior is largely due to the towers with which it was adorned. The most massive tower was ordinarily one which stood, like the central one of Lichfield Cathedral, at the crossing of the nave and transepts. Two towers were usually intended at the western front of the building, and sometimes one, or occasionally two, at the end of each transept. It is rare to find a cathedral where the whole of these towers have been even begun, much less completed. In many cases only one, in others three, have been built. In some instances they have been erected, and have fallen. In others they have never been carried up at all. During a large portion of the Gothic period it was usual to add to each tower a lofty pyramidal roof or spire, and these are still standing in some instances, though many of them have disappeared. Occasionally a tower was built quite detached from the church to which it belonged.

To cathedrals and abbey churches a group of monastic buildings was appended. It will not be necessary to describe these in much detail. They were grouped round an open square, surrounded by a vaulted and arcaded passage, which is known as the cloister. This was usually fitted into the warm and sheltered angle formed by the south side of the nave and the south transept, though occasionally the cloister is found on the north side of the nave. The most important building opening out of the cloister is the chapter-house, frequently a lofty and richly-ornamented room, often octagonal, and generally standing south of the south transept. The usual arrangement of the monastic buildings round and adjoining the cloister varied in details with the requirements of the different monastic orders, and the circumstances of each individual religious house, but, as in the case of churches, the general principles of disposition were fixed early. They are embodied in a manuscript plan, dating as far back as the ninth century, and found at St. Gall in Switzerland, and never seem to have been widely departed from. The monks' dormitory here occupies the whole east side of the great cloister, there being no chapter-house. It is usually met with as nearly in this position as the transept and the chapter-house will permit. The refectory is on the south side of the cloister, and has a connected kitchen. The west side of the cloister in this instance was occupied by a great cellar. Frequently a hospitium, or apartment for entertaining guests, stood here. The north side of the cloister was formed by the church.

For the abbot a detached house was provided in the St. Gall plan to stand on

---

[2] At E on the plan of Peterborough (Fig. 2).
[3] See Glossary.

the north side of the church; and a second superior hospitum for his guests. Eastward of the church are placed the infirmary with its chapel, and an infirmarer's lodging. The infirmary was commonly arranged with a nave and aisles, much like, a small parish church. Other detached buildings gave a public school, a school for novices with its chapel, and, more remotely placed, granaries, mills, a bakehouse, and other offices. A garden and a cemetery formed part of the scheme, which corresponds tolerably well with that of many monastic buildings remaining in England, as *e.g.*, those at Fountains' Abbey, Furness Abbey, or Westminster Abbey, so far as they can be traced.

Generally speaking the principal buildings in a monastery were long and not very wide apartments, with windows on both sides. Frequently they were vaulted, and they often had a row of columns down the middle. Many are two stories high. Of the dependencies, the kitchen, which was often a vaulted apartment with a chimney, and the barn, which was often of great size, were the most prominent. They are often fine buildings. At Glastonbury very good examples of a monastic barn and kitchen can be seen.

Second only in importance to the churches and religious buildings come the military and domestic buildings of the Gothic period (Fig. 7).

FIG. 7.—HOUSE OF JAQUES CŒUR AT BOURGES. (BEGUN 1413.)

Every dwelling-house of consequence was more or less fortified, at any rate during the twelfth, thirteenth, and fourteenth centuries. A lofty square tower, called a keep, built to stand a siege, and with a walled inclosure at its feet, often protected by a wide ditch (fosse or moat), formed the castle of the twelfth century, and in some cases (*e.g.* the White Tower of London), this keep was of considerable size. The first step in enlargement was to increase the number and importance of the buildings which clustered round the keep, and to form two inclosures for them, known as an inner and an outer bailey. The outer buildings of the Tower of London, though much modernised, will give a good idea of what a first class castle grew to be by successive additions of this sort. In castles erected near the end of the thirteenth century (*e.g.* Conway Castle in North Wales), and later, the square form of the keep was abandoned, and many more arrangements for the comfort and convenience of the occupants were introduced; and the buildings and additions to buildings of the fifteenth century took more the shape of a modern dwelling-house, partly protected against violence, but by no means strong enough to stand a siege. Penshurst may be cited as a good example of this class of building.

It will be understood that, unlike the religious buildings which early received the form and disposition from which they did not depart widely, mediæval domestic buildings exhibit an amount of change in which we can readily trace the effects of the gradual settlement of this country, the abandonment of habits of petty warfare, the ultimate cessation of civil wars, the introduction of gunpowder, the increase in wealth and desire for comfort, and last, but not least, the confiscation by Henry VIII. of the property of the monastic houses.

FIG. 8.—PLAN OF WARWICK CASTLE. (14TH AND FOLLOWING CENTURIES.)

Warwick Castle, of which we give a plan (Fig. 8), maybe cited as a good example of an English castellated mansion of the time of Richard II. Below the principal story there is a vaulted basement containing the kitchens and many of the offices. On the main floor we find the hall, entered as usual at the lower or servants' end, from a porch. The upper end gives access to a sitting-room, built immediately behind it, and beyond are a drawing-room and state bed-rooms, while across a passage are placed the private chapel and a large dining-room (a modern addition). Bed-rooms occupy the upper floors of the buildings at both ends of the hall.

Perhaps even more interesting as a study than Warwick Castle is Haddon Hall, the well-preserved residence of the Duke of Rutland, in Derbyshire. The five or six successive enlargements and additions which this building has received between the thirteenth and seventeenth centuries show the growth of ideas of comfort and even luxury in this country.

As it now stands, Haddon Hall contains two internal quadrangles, separated from one another by the great hall with its dais, its minstrels' gallery, its vast open fire-place, and its traceried windows, and by the kitchens, butteries, &c., belonging to it.

The most important apartments are reached from the upper end of the hall, and consist of the magnificent ball-room, and a dining-room in the usual position, *i.e.* adjoining the hall and opening out of it; with, on the upper floor, a drawing-room, and a suite of state bed-rooms, occupying the south side of both quadrangles and the east end of one. A large range of apartments, added at a late period, and many of them finely panelled and lined with tapestry, occupies the north side of this building and the northwestern tower. At the south-western corner of the building stands a chapel of considerable size, and which once seems to have served as a kind of parochial church; and a very considerable number of rooms of small size, opening out of both quadrangles, would afford shelter, if not comfortable lodging, to retainers, servants, and others. The portions built in the thirteenth, fourteenth, and fifteenth centuries are more or less fortified. The ball-room, which is of Elizabethan architecture, opens on to a terraced garden, accessible from without by no more violent means than climbing over a not very formidable wall. Probably nowhere in England, can the growth of domestic architecture be better studied, whether we look to the alterations which took place in accommodation and arrangement, or to the changes which occurred in the architectural treatment of windows, battlements, doorways and other features, than at Haddon Hall.

FIG. 9.—PALACES ON THE GRAND CANAL, VENICE. (14TH CEN-
TURY.)

In towns and cities much beautiful domestic architecture is to be found in the
ordinary dwelling-houses, *e.g.* houses from Chester and Lisieux (Figs. 14 and 15);
but many specimens have of course perished, especially as timber was freely used

in their construction. Dwelling-houses of a high order of excellence, and of large size, were also built during this period. The Gothic palaces of Venice, of which many stand on the Grand Canal (Fig. 9), are the best examples of these, and the lordly Ducal Palace in that city is perhaps the finest secular building which exists of Gothic architecture.

Municipal buildings of great size and beauty are to be found in North Italy and Germany, but chiefly in Belgium, where the various town-halls of Louvain, Bruges, Ypres, Ghent, Antwerp, Brussels, &c., vie with each other in magnificence and extent.

Many secular buildings also remain to us of which the architecture is Gothic. Among these we find public halls and large buildings for public purposes—as Westminster Hall, or the Palace of Justice at Rouen; hospitals, as that at Milan; or colleges, as King's College, Cambridge, with its unrivalled chapel. Many charming minor works, such as fountains, wells (Fig. 10), crosses, tombs, monuments, and the fittings of the interior of churches, also remain to attest the versatility, the power of design, and the cultivated taste of the architects of the Gothic period.

FIG. 10.—WELL AT REGENSBURG, (15TH CENTURY.)

**FIG. 11.—GOTHIC ORNAMENT. FROM SENS CATHEDRAL
(HEADPIECE)**

CHAPTER III.

GOTHIC ARCHITECTURE IN GREAT BRITAIN.

ENGLISH Gothic architecture has been usually subdivided into three periods or stages of advancement, corresponding to those enumerated on page 1;
the early stage known as Early English, or sometimes as Lancet, occupying the
thirteenth century and something more; the middle stage, known as Decorated,
occupying most of the fourteenth century; and the latest stage, known as Perpendicular, occupying the fifteenth century and part of the sixteenth.

The duration of each of these coincides approximately with the century, the
transition from each phase to the next taking place chiefly in the last quarter of the
century. Adding the periods of the English types of round arched Architecture, we
obtain the following table:—

Up to 1066 or up to middle of 11th century, Saxon.

A.D. 1066 to 1189 or up to end of 12th century, Norman.

A.D. 1189 to 1307 or up to end of 13th century, Early English.

A.D. 1307 to 1377 or up to end of 14th century, Decorated.

A.D. 1377 to 1546 or up to middle of 16th century, Perpendicular.

The term "Early English" (short for Early English Gothic) applied to English
thirteenth-century architecture explains itself.

The term "Lancet" sometimes applied to the Early English style, is derived
from the shape of the ordinary window-heads, which resemble the point of a lan-

cet in outline (Fig. 16). Whatever term be adopted, it is necessary to remark that a wide difference exists between the earlier and the late examples of this period. It will suffice for our purposes if, when speaking of the fully-developed style of the late examples, we refer to it as Advanced Early English.

The architecture of the fourteenth century is called "Decorated," from the great increase of ornament, especially in window tracery and carved enrichments.

The architecture of the fifteenth century is called "Perpendicular," from the free use made of perpendicular lines, both in general features and in ornaments, especially in the tracery of the windows and the panelling with which walls are ornamented.[4]

The following condensed list, partly from Morant,[5] of the most striking peculiarities of each period, may be found useful for reference, and is on that account placed here, notwithstanding that it contains many technical words, for the meaning of which the student must consult the Glossary which forms part of this volume.

ANGLO-SAXON — (Prior to the Norman Conquest). —

Rude work and rough material; walls mostly of rubble or ragstone with ashlar at the angles in long and short courses alternately; openings with round or triangular heads, sometimes divided by a rude baluster. Piers plain, square, and narrow. Windows splayed externally and internally. Rude square blocks of stone in place of capitals and bases. Mouldings generally semi-cylindrical and coarsely chiselled. Corners of buildings square without buttresses.

NORMAN.	William I.	A.D.	1066.
	William II.	″	1087.
	Henry I.	″	1100.
	Stephen	″	1135.
	Henry II.	″	1154 to 1189.

Arches semicircular, occasionally stilted; at first plain, afterwards enriched with chevron or other mouldings; and frequent repetition of same ornament on each stone. Piers low and massive, cylindrical, square, polygonal, or composed of clustered shafts, often ornamented with spiral bands and mouldings. Windows generally narrow and splayed internally only; sometimes double and divided by a shaft. Walls sometimes a series of arcades, a few pierced as windows, the rest left blank. Doorways deeply recessed and richly ornamented with bands of mouldings. Doors often square headed, but under arches the head of the arch filled with carving. Capitals carved in outline, often grotesquely sculptured with devices of animals and leaves. Abacus square, lower edge moulded. Bases much resembling the classic orders. The mouldings at first imperfectly formed. Pedestals of piers square. Buttresses plain, with broad faces and small projections. Parapets plain

---

[4] The abbreviations, E. E., Dec., and Perp., will be employed to denote these three periods.

[5] *Notes on English Architecture, Costumes, Monuments, &c. Privately printed.* Quoted here with the author's permission.

with projecting corbel table under.

Plain mouldings consist of chamfers, round or pointed rolls at edges, divided from plain face by shallow channels. Enriched mouldings—the chevrons or zig-zag, the billet square or round, the cable, the lozenge, the chain, nail heads, and others. Niches with figures over doorways. Roofs of moderately high pitch, and open to the frame; timbers chiefly king-post trusses. Towers square and massive—those of late date richly adorned with arcades. Openings in towers often beautifully grouped. Vaulting waggon-headed, and simple intersecting vaults of semicircular outline.

Towards the close of the style in reign of Henry II., details of transitional character begin to appear. Pointed arch with Norman pier. Arcades of intersecting semicircular arches. Norman abacus blended with Early English foliage in capitals.

Early English.   Richard I.   A.D.   1189 *Transition.*
John   "   1199.
Henry III.   "   1216.
Edward I.   "   1272 to 1307.

General proportions more slender, and height of walls, columns, &c., greater. Arches pointed, generally lancet; often richly moulded. Triforium arches and arcades open with trefoiled heads. Piers slender, composed of a central circular shaft surrounded by several smaller ones, almost or quite detached; generally with horizontal bands. In small buildings plain polygonal and circular piers are used. Capitals concave in outline, moulded, or carved with conventional foliage delicately executed and arranged vertically. The abacus always undercut. Detached shafts often of Purbeck marble. Base a deep hollow between two rounds. Windows at first long, narrow, and deeply splayed internally, the glass within a few inches of outer face of wall; later in the style less acute, divided by mullions, enriched with cusped circles in the head, often of three or more lights, the centre light being the highest. Doorways often deeply recessed and enriched with slender shafts and elaborate mouldings. Shafts detached. Buttresses about equal in projection to width, with but one set-off, or without any. Buttresses at angles always in pairs. Mouldings bold and deeply undercut, consisting chiefly of round mouldings sometimes pointed or with a fillett, separated by deep hollows. Great depth of moulded surface generally arranged on rectangular planes. Hollows of irregular curve sometimes filled with dogtooth ornament or with foliage. Roofs of high pitch, timbers plain, and where there is no vault open.

Early in the style finials were plain bunches of leaves; towards the close beautifully carved finials and crockets with carved foliage of conventional character were introduced. Flat surfaces often richly diapered. Spires broached. Vaulting pointed with diagonal and main ribs only; ridge ribs not introduced till late in the style; bosses at intersection of ribs.

Decorated.   Edward II.   A.D.   1307.
Edward III.   "   1377 to 1379.

Proportions less lofty than in the previous style. Arches mostly inclosing an equilateral angle, the mouldings often continued down the pier. Windows large, and divided into two or more lights by mullions. Tracery in the head, at first composed geometrical forms, later of flowing character. Clerestory windows generally small. Diamond shaped piers with shafts engaged. Capitals with scroll moulding on under side of abacus, with elegant foliage arranged horizontally. Doors frequently without shafts, the arch moulding running down the jambs. Rich doorways and windows often surrounded with triangular and ogee-shaped canopies. Buttresses in stages variously ornamented. Parapet pierced with quatrefoils and flowing tracery. Niches panelled and with projecting canopies. Spires lofty; the broach rarely used, parapets and angle pinnacles take the place of it. Roofs of moderate pitch open to the framing. Mouldings bold and finely proportioned, generally in groups, the groups separated from each other by hollows, composed of segments of circles. Deep hollows, now generally confined to inner angles. Mouldings varying in size and kind, arranged on diagonal as well as rectangular planes, often ornamented with ball flower. Foliage chiefly of ivy, oak, and vine leaves; natural, also conventional. Rich crockets, finials, and pinnacles. Vaulting with intermediate ribs, ridge ribs, and late in the style lierne ribs, and bosses.

PERPENDICULAR.	Richard II.	A.D.	1377. (*Transition.*)
	Henry IV.	"	1399.
	Henry V.	"	1413.
	Henry VI.	"	1422.
	Edward IV.	"	1461.
	Edward V.	"	1483.
	Richard III.	"	1483.
TUDOR.	Henry VII.	"	1485.
	Henry VIII.	"	1509 to 1546.

Arches at first inclosing an equilateral triangle, afterwards obtusely pointed and struck from four centres. Piers generally oblong; longitudinal direction north and south. Mouldings continued from base through arch. Capitals with mouldings large, angular, and few, with abacus and bell imperfectly defined. Foliage of conventional character, shallow, and square in outline. Bases polygonal. Windows where lofty divided into stories by transoms. The mullions often continued perpendicularly into the head. Canopies of ogee character enriched with crockets. Doors generally with square label over arch, the spandrels filled with ornament. Buttresses with bold projection often ending in finials. Flying buttresses pierced with tracery. Walls profusely ornamented with panelling. Parapets embattled and panelled. Open timber roofs of moderate pitch, of elaborate construction, often with hammer beams, richly ornamented with moulded timbers, carved figures of angels and with pierced tracery in spandrels. Roofs sometimes of very flat pitch. Lofty clerestories. Mouldings large, coarse, and with wide and shallow hollows and hard wiry edges, meagre in appearance and wanting in minute and delicate detail, generally arranged on diagonal planes. Early in the style the mouldings partake of decorated character.

In the Tudor period depressed four-centered arch prevails; transoms of windows battlemented. Tudor flower, rose, portcullis, and fleur-de-lis common ornaments. Crockets and pinnacles much projected. Roofs of low pitch.

Vaulting. Fan vaulting, with tracery and pendants elaborately carved.

Other modes of distinguishing the periods of English Gothic have been proposed by writers of authority. The division given above is that of Rickman, and is generally adopted. A more minute subdivision and a different set of names were proposed by Sharpe as follows:—

ROMANESQUE.	Saxon	A.D.	to 1066.
	Norman	"	1066 to 1145.
GOTHIC.	Transitional	"	1145 to 1190.
	Lancet	"	1190 to 1245.
	Geometrical	"	1245 to 1315.
	Curvilinear	"	1315 to 1360.
	Rectilinear	"	1360 to 1550.

Of the new names proposed by Mr. Sharpe "transitional" explains itself; and "geometrical, curvilinear, and rectilinear" refer to the characters of the window tracery at the different periods which they denote.[6]

The history of English Gothic proper may be said to begin with the reign of Henry II., coinciding very nearly with the commencement of the period named by Mr. Sharpe transitional (1145 to 1190), when Norman architecture was changing into Gothic. This history we propose now to consider somewhat in detail, dividing the buildings in the simplest possible way, namely, into floors, walls, columns, roofs, openings, and ornaments. After this we shall have to consider the mode in which materials were used by the builders of the Gothic period, *i.e.* the construction of the buildings; and the general artistic principles which guided their architects, *i.e.* the design of the buildings.

It may be useful to students in and near London to give Sir G. Gilbert Scott's list of striking London examples[7] of Gothic architecture (with the omission of such examples as are more antiquarian than architectural in their interest):—

Norman (temp. Conquest).—The Keep and Chapel of the Tower of London.

Advanced Norman.—Chapel of St. Catherine, Westminster Abbey; St. Bartholomew's Priory, Smithfield.

Transitional.—The round part of the Temple Church.

Early English.—Eastern part of the Temple Church; Choir and Lady Chapel of St. Mary Overy, Southwark; Chapel of Lambeth Palace.

---

[6] See examples in Chapter V. and in Glossary.
[7] Address to Conference of Architects, *Builder*, June 24, 1876.

Advanced Early English (passing to decorated).—Eastern part of Westminster Abbey generally and its Chapter House.

Early Decorated.—Choir of Westminster, (but this has been much influenced by the design of the earlier parts adjacent); Chapel of St. Etheldreda, Ely Place, Holborn.

Late Decorated.—The three bays of the Cloister at Westminster opposite the entrance to Chapter House; Crypt of St. Stephen's Chapel, Westminster; Dutch Church, Austin Friars.

Early Perpendicular.—South and West walks of the Cloister, Westminster; Westminster Hall.

Advanced Perpendicular (Tudor period).—Henry VII.'s Chapel; Double Cloister of St. Stephen's, Westminster.

CHAPTER IV.

GOTHIC ARCHITECTURE.—ENGLAND.

Analysis of buildings.—Floor, walls, towers, gables, columns.

Floor, or Plan.

THE excellences or defects of a building are more due to the shape and size of its floor and, incidentally, of the walls and columns or piers which inclose and subdivide its floor than to anything else whatever. A map of the floor and walls (usually showing also the position of the doors and windows), is known as a plan, but by a pardonable figure of speech the plan of a building is often understood to mean the shape and size and arrangement of its floor and walls themselves, instead of simply the drawing representing them. It is in this sense that the word plan will be used in this volume.

The plan of a Gothic Cathedral has been described, and it has been already remarked that before the Gothic period had commenced the dimensions of great churches had been very much increased. The generally received disposition of the parts of a church had indeed been already settled or nearly so. There were consequently few radical alterations in church plans during the Gothic period. One, however, took place in England in the abandonment of the apse.

At first the apsidal east end, common in the Norman times, was retained. For example, it is found at Canterbury, where the choir and transept are transitional, having been begun soon after 1174 and completed about 1184; but the eastern end of Chichester, which belongs to the same period (the transition), displays the square east end, and this termination was almost invariably preferred in our country after the twelfth century.

A great amount of regularity marks the plans of those great churches which had vaulted roofs, as will be readily understood when it is remembered that the vaults were divided into equal and similar compartments, and that the points of support had to be placed with corresponding regularity. Where, however, some controlling cause of this nature was not at work much picturesque irregularity prevailed in the planning of English Gothic buildings of all periods. The plans of our Cathedrals are noted for their great length in proportion to their width, for the considerable length given to the transepts, and for the occurrence in many cases (*e.g.* Salisbury, thirteenth century) of a second transept. The principal alterations which took place in plan as time went on originated in the desire to concentrate material as much as possible on points of support, leaving the walls between them thin and the openings wide, and in the use of flying buttresses, the feet of which occupy a considerable space outside the main walls of the church. The plans of piers and columns also underwent the alterations which will be presently described.[8]

Buildings of a circular shape on plan are very rare, but octagonal ones are not uncommon. The finest chapter-houses attached to our Cathedrals are octagons, with a central pier to carry the vaulting. On the whole, play of shape on plan was less cultivated in England than in some continental countries.

The plans of domestic buildings are usually simple, but grew more elaborate and extensive as time went on. The cloister with dwelling-rooms and common-rooms entered from its walk, formed the model on which colleges, hospitals, and alms-houses were planned. The castle, already described, was the residence of the wealthy during the earlier part of the Gothic period, and when, in the fourteenth and fifteenth centuries, houses which were rather dwellings than fortresses began to be erected, the hall, with a large bay window and a raised floor or dais at one end and a mighty open fire-place, was always the most conspicuous feature in the plan. Towards the close of the Gothic period the plan of a great dwelling, such as Warwick Castle (Fig. 8), began to show many of the features which distinguish a mansion of the present day.

In various parts of the country remains of magnificent Gothic dwelling-houses of the fourteenth and fifteenth centuries exist, and long before the close of the perpendicular period we had such mansions as Penshurst and Hever, such palaces as Windsor and Wells, such castellated dwellings as Warwick and Haddon, differing in many respects but all agreeing in the possession of a great central hall. Buildings for public purposes also often took the form of a great hall. Westminster Hall may be cited as the finest example of such a structure, not only in England but in Europe.

The student who desires to obtain anything beyond the most superficial acquaintance with architecture must endeavour to obtain enough familiarity with ground plans, to be able to sketch, measure, and lay down a plan to scale and to *read* one. The plan shows to the experienced architect the nature, arrangement, and qualities of a building better than any other drawing, and a better memorandum of a building is preserved if a fairly correct sketch of its plan, or of the plan of important parts of it, is preserved than if written notes are alone relied upon.

[8] For illustrations consult the Glossary under *Pier*.

Walls.

The walls of Gothic buildings are generally of stone; brick being the exception. They were in the transitional and Early English times extremely thick, and became thinner afterwards. All sorts of ornamental masonry were introduced into them, so that diapers,[9] bands, arcades, mouldings, and inlaid patterns are all to be met with occasionally, especially in districts where building materials of varied colours, or easy to work, are plentiful. In the perpendicular period the walls were systematically covered with panelling closely resembling the tracery of the windows (*e.g.*, Henry VII.'s Chapel at Westminster).

The wall of a building ordinarily requires some kind of base and some kind of top. The base or plinth in English Gothic buildings was usually well marked and bold, especially in the perpendicular period, and it is seldom absent. The eaves of the roof in some cases overhang the walls, resting on a simple stone band, called an eaves-course, and constitute the crowning feature. In many instances, however, the eaves are concealed behind a parapet[10] which is often carried on a moulded cornice or on corbels. This, in the E. E. period, was usually very simple. In the Dec. it was panelled with ornamental panels, and often made very beautiful. In the Perp. it was frequently battlemented as well as panelled.

A distinguishing feature of Gothic walls is the buttress. It existed, but only in the form of a flat pier of very slight projection in Norman, as in almost all Romanesque buildings, but in the Gothic period it became developed.

The buttress, like many of the peculiarities of Gothic architecture, originated in the use of stone vaults and the need for strong piers at these points, upon which the thrust and weight of those vaults were concentrated. The use of very large openings, for wide windows full of stained glass also made it increasingly necessary in the Dec. and Perp. periods to fortify the walls at regular points.

A buttress[11] is, in fact, a piece of wall set athwart the main wall, usually projecting considerably at the base and diminished by successive reductions of its mass as it approaches the top, and so placed as to counteract the thrust of some arch or vault inside. It had great artistic value; in the feeble and level light of our Northern climate it casts bold shadows and catches bright lights, and so adds greatly to the architectural effect of the exterior. In the E. E. the buttress was simple and ordinarily projected about its own width. In the Dec. it obtained much more projection, was constructed with several diminutions (technically called weatherings), and was considerably ornamented. In the Perp. it was frequently enriched by panelling. The buttresses in the Dec. period are often set diagonally at the corner of a building or tower. In the E. E. period this was never done.

The flying buttress[12] is one of the most conspicuous features of the exterior of those Gothic buildings which possessed elaborate stone vaults. It was a contrivance for providing an abutment to counterbalance the outward pressure of the

[9] For illustration consult the Glossary.
[10] For illustrations consult the Glossary.
[11] For illustrations consult the Glossary.
[12] For illustration consult the Glossary under *Flying buttress.*

vault covering the highest and central parts of the building in cases where that vault rested upon and abutted against walls which themselves were carried by arches, and were virtually internal walls, so that no buttress could be carried up from the ground to steady them.

A pier of masonry, sometimes standing alone, sometimes thrown out from the aisle wall opposite the point to be propped, formed the solid part of this buttress; it was carried to the requisite height and a flying arch spanning the whole width of the aisles was thrown across from it to the wall at the point whence the vault sprung. The pier itself was in many cases loaded by an enormous pinnacle, so that its weight might combine with the pressure transmitted along the slope of the flying arch to give a resultant which should fall within the base of the buttress. The back of such an arch was generally used as a water channel.

The forest of flying buttresses round many French cathedrals produces an almost bewildering effect, as, for instance, at the east end of Notre Dame;—our English specimens, at Westminster Abbey for example, are comparatively simple.

Towers.

The gable and the tower are developments of the walls of the building. Gothic is *par excellence* the style of towers. Many towers were built detached from all other buildings, but no great Gothic building is complete without one main tower and some subordinate ones.

In the E. E. style church towers were often crowned by low spires, becoming more lofty as the style advanced. In the Dec. style lofty spires were almost universal. In the Perp. the tower rarely has a visible roof.[13]

The artistic value of towers in giving unity coupled with variety to a group of buildings can hardly be exaggerated.

The positions which towers occupy are various. They produce the greatest effect when central, *i.e.* placed over the crossing of the nave and transepts. Lichfield, Chichester, and Salisbury may be referred to as examples of cathedrals with towers in this position and surmounted by spires. Canterbury, York, Lincoln, and Gloucester are specimens of the effectiveness of the tower similarly placed, but without a spire (Fig. 12). At Wells a fine central octagon occupies the crossing, and is remarkable for the skill with which it is fitted to the nave and aisles internally. Next to central towers rank a pair of towers at the western end of the building. These exist at Lichfield with their spires; they exist (square-topped) at Lincoln, and (though carried up since the Gothic period) at Westminster.[14] Many churches have a single tower in this position (Fig. 13).

The obvious purpose of a tower, beyond its serviceableness as a feature of the building and as a landmark, is to lift up a belfry high into the air: accordingly, almost without exception, church and cathedral towers are designed with a large upper story, pierced by openings of great size and height called the belfry stage;

---

[13] For remarks on Spires, see Chap. V.

[14] York, Lichfield, and Lincoln, are the cathedrals distinguished by the possession of three towers.

and the whole artistic treatment of the tower is subordinate to this feature. It is also very often the case that a turret to contain a spiral staircase which may afford the means of access to the upper part of the tower, forms a prominent feature of its whole height, especially in the Dec. and Perp. periods.

FIG. 12.—LINCOLN CATHEDRAL. (MOSTLY EARLY ENGLISH.)

In domestic and monastic buildings, low towers were frequently employed with excellent effect. Many castles retained the Norman keep, or square strong tower, which had served as the nucleus round which other buildings had afterwards clustered; but where during the Gothic period a castle was built, or rebuilt, without such a keep, one or more towers, often of great beauty, were always added. Examples abound; good ones will be found in the Edwardian castles in Wales (end of thirteenth century), as for example at Conway and Caernarvon.

Gables.

The gable forms a distinctive Gothic feature. The gables crowned those parts of a great church in which the skill of the architect was directed to producing a regular composition, often called a front, or a façade. The west fronts of Cathedrals were the most important architectural designs of this sort, and with them we may include the ends of the transepts and the east fronts.

The same parts of parish churches are often excellent compositions. The gable of the nave always formed the central feature of the main front. This was flanked by the gables, or half-gables, of the aisles where there were no towers, or by the lower portions of the towers. As a rule the centre and sides of the façade are separated by buttresses, or some other mode of marking a vertical division, and the composition is also divided by bands of mouldings or otherwise, horizontally into storeys. Some of the horizontal divisions are often strongly marked, especially in the lower part of the building, where in early examples there is sometimes in addition to the plinth, or base of the wall, an arcade or a band of sculpture running across the entire front (*e.g.* east front of Lincoln Cathedral). The central gable is always occupied by a large window—or in early buildings a group of windows— sometimes two storeys in height. A great side window usually occurs at the end of each aisle. Below these great windows are introduced, at any rate in west fronts, the doorways, which, even in the finest English examples, are comparatively small. The gable also contains as a rule one or more windows often circular which light the space above the vaults.

FIG. 13.—ST. PIERRE, CAEN, TOWER AND SPIRE. (SPIRE, 1302.)

Part of the art in arranging such a composition is to combine and yet contrast its horizontal and vertical elements. The horizontal lines, or features, are those which serve to bind the whole together, and the vertical ones are those which give that upward tendency which is the great charm and peculiar characteristic of Gothic architecture. It is essential for the masses of solid masonry and the openings to be properly contrasted and proportioned to each other, and here, as in every part of a building, such ornaments and ornamental features as are introduced must be designed to contribute to the enrichment of the building as a whole, so that no part shall be conspicuous either by inharmonious treatment, undue plainness, or excessive enrichment.

FIG. 14.—HOUSE AT CHESTER. (16TH CENTURY.)

During the transition the gable became steeper in pitch than the comparatively moderate slope of Norman times. In the E. E. it was acutely pointed, in the Dec. the usual slope was that of the two sides of an equilateral triangle: in the Perp. it became extremely flat and ceased to be so marked a feature as it had formerly been. In domestic buildings the gable was employed in the most effective manner, and town dwelling-houses were almost invariably built their gable ends to the street (Fig. 14).

A very effective form of wall was frequently made use of in dwelling-houses. This consisted of a sturdy framework of stout timbers exposed to view, with the spaces between them filled in with plaster. Of this work, which is known as half-timbered work, many beautiful specimens remain dating from the fifteenth and following centuries (Figs. 14 and 15), and a few of earlier date. In those parts of England where tiles are manufactured such framework was often covered by tiles instead of being filled in with plastering. In half-timbered houses, the fire-places and chimneys, and sometimes also the basement storeys, are usually of brickwork or masonry; so are the side walls in the case of houses in streets. It was usual in such buildings to cause the upper storeys to overhang the lower ones.

Columns and Piers.

The columns and piers of a building virtually form portions of its walls, so far as aiding to support the weight of the roof is concerned, and are appropriately considered in connection with them. In Gothic architecture very little use is made of columns on the outside of a building, and the porticoes and external rows of columns proper to the classic styles are quite unknown. On the other hand the series of piers, or columns, from which spring the arches which separate the central avenues of nave, transepts and choir from the aisles, are among the most prominent features in every church. These piers varied in each century.[15]

The Norman piers had been frequently circular or polygonal, but sometimes nearly square, and usually of enormous mass. Thus, at Durham (Norman), oblong piers of about eleven feet in diameter occur alternately with round ones of about seven feet. In transitional examples columns of more slender proportions were employed either (as in the choir of Canterbury) as single shafts or collected into groups. Where grouping took place it was intended that each shaft of the group should be seen to support some definite feature of the superincumbent structure, as where a separate group of mouldings springs from each shaft in a doorway, and this principle was very steadily adhered to during the greater part of the Gothic period.[16]

---

[15] For illustrations consult the Glossary under *Pier*.
[16] For illustrations consult the Glossary under *Pier*.

FIG. 15.—HOUSES AT LISIEUX, FRANCE. (16TH CENTURY.)

Through the E. E. period groups of shafts are generally employed; they are often formed of detached shafts clustering round a central one, and held together at intervals by bands or belts of masonry, and generally the entire group is nearly circular on plan. In the succeeding century (Dec. period) the piers also take the form of groups of shafts, but they are generally carved out of one block of stone, and the ordinary arrangement of the pier is on a lozenge-shaped plan. In the Perp., the piers retain the same general character, but are slenderer, and the shafts have often shrunk to nothing more than reedy mouldings.

The column is often employed in Transitional and E. E. churches as a substitute for piers carrying arches. In every period small columns are freely used as ornamental features. They are constantly met with, for example, in the jambs of doorways and of windows.

Every column is divided naturally into three parts, its base, or foot; its shaft, which forms the main body; and its capital, or head. Each of these went through a series of modifications. Part of the base usually consisted of a flat stone larger than the diameter of the column, sometimes called a plinth, and upon this stood the moulded base which gradually diminished to the size of the shaft. This plain stone was in E. E. often square, and in that case the corner spaces which were not covered by the mouldings of the base were often occupied by an elegantly carved leaf. In Dec. and Perp. buildings the lower part of the base was often polygonal, and frequently moulded so as to make it into a pedestal.[17]

The proportions of shafts varied extraordinarily; they were, as a rule, extremely slender when their purpose was purely decorative, and comparatively sturdy when they really served to carry a weight.

The capital of the column has been perhaps the most conspicuous feature in the architecture of every age and every country, and it is one of the features which a student may make use of as an indication of date and style of buildings, very much as the botanist employs the flower as an index to the genus and species of plants. The capital almost invariably starts from a ring, called the neck of the column. This serves to mark the end of the shaft and the commencement of the capital. Above this follows what is commonly called the bell,—the main portion of the capital, which is that part upon which the skill of the carver and the taste of the designer can be most freely expended, and on the top of the bell is placed the abacus, a flat block of stone upon the upper surface of which is built the superstructure or is laid the beam or block which the column has to support. The shape and ornaments given to the abacus are often of considerable importance as indications of the position in architectural history which the building in which it occurs should occupy.

The Norman capital differed to some extent from the Romanesque capitals of other parts of Europe. It was commonly of a heavy, strong-looking shape, and is often appropriately called the cushion capital. In its simpler forms the cushion capital is nothing but a cubical block of stone with its lower corners rounded off to make it fit the circular shaft on which it is placed, and with a slab by way of abacus placed upon it. In later Norman and transitional work the faces of this block and the edges of the abacus are often richly moulded. By degrees, however, as the transition to E. E. approached, a new sort of capital[18] was introduced, having the outline of the bell hollow instead of convex. The square faces of the Norman capital of course disappeared, and the square abacus soon (at least in this country) became circular, involving no small loss of vigour in the appearance of the work. The bell

[17] For illustrations consult the Glossary under *Base*.
[18] For illustrations consult the Glossary.

of this capital was often decorated with rich mouldings, and had finely-designed and characteristic foliage, which almost always seemed to grow up the capital, and represented a conventional kind of leaf easily recognised when once seen.

In the Dec. period the capitals have, as a rule, fewer and less elaborate mouldings; the foliage is often very beautifully carved in imitation of natural leaves, and wreathed round the capital instead of growing up it. In the Perp. this feature is in every way less ornate, the mouldings are plainer, and the foliage, often absent, is, when it occurs, conventional and stiff. Polygonal capitals are common in this period.

LATER NORMAN CAPITAL.

CHAPTER V.

GOTHIC ARCHITECTURE.—ENGLAND.

Analysis of buildings (continued)—openings, roofs, spires, ornaments, stained glass, sculpture.

Openings and Arches.

THE openings (*i.e.* doors and windows) in the walls of English Gothic buildings are occasionally covered by flat heads or lintels, but this is exceptional; ordinarily they have arched heads. The shape of the arch varies at all periods. Architects always felt themselves free to adopt any shape which best met the requirements of any special case; but at each period there was one shape of arch which it was customary to use.

In the first transitional period (end of twelfth century) semicircular and pointed arches are both met with, and are often both employed in the same part of the same building. The mouldings and enrichments which are common in Norman work are usually still in use. In the E. E. period the doorways are almost invariably rather acutely pointed, the arched heads are enriched by a large mass of rich mouldings, and the jambs[19] have usually a series of small columns, each of which is intended to carry a portion of the entire group of mouldings. Large doorways are often subdivided into two, and frequently approached by porches. A most beautiful example occurs in the splendid west entrance to Ely Cathedral. Other examples will be found at Lichfield (Fig. 1) and Salisbury. It was not uncommon to cover doorways with a lintel, the whole being under an archway; this left a space above the head of the door which was occupied by carving often of great beauty. Ornamental gables are often formed over the entrances of churches, and are richly sculptured; but though beautiful, these features rarely attained magnificence. The most remarkable entrance to an English cathedral is the west portal of Peterborough—a composition of lofty and richly moulded arches built in front of the original west wall. A portal on a smaller scale, but added in the same manner adorns the west front of Wells. As a less exceptional example we may refer to the entrance to Westminster Abbey at the end of the north transept (now under restoration),

[19] For illustrations consult the Glossary under *Jamb*.

which must have been a noble example of an E. E. portal when in its perfect state.

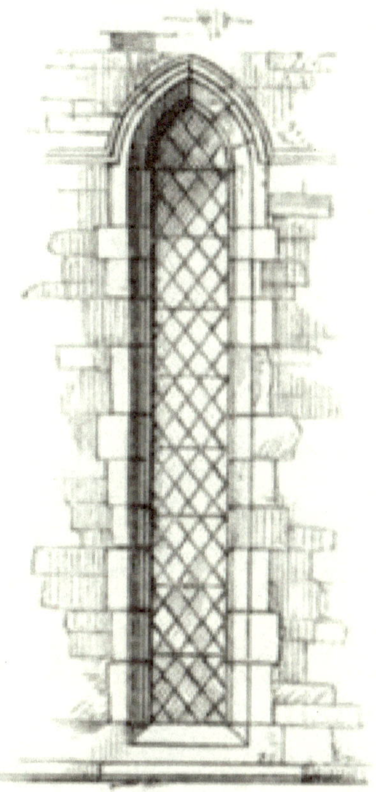

FIG. 16.—LANCET WINDOW. (12TH CENTURY.)

The windows in this style were almost always long, narrow, and with a pointed head resembling the blade of a lancet (Fig. 16). The glass is generally near the outside face of the wall, and the sides of the opening are splayed towards the inside. It was very customary to place these lancet windows in groups. The best known group is the celebrated one of "the five sisters," five lofty single lights, occupying the eastern end of one of the transepts of York Minster. A common arrangement in designing such a group was to make the central light the highest, and to graduate the height of the others. It after a time became customary to render the opening more ornamental by adding pointed projections called cusps. By these the shape of the head of the opening was turned into a form resembling a trefoil leaf. Sometimes two cusps were added on each side. The head is, in the former case, said to be trefoiled—in the latter, cinqfoiled.

FIG. 17.—TWO-LIGHT WINDOW. (13TH CENTURY.)

FIG. 18.—GEOMETRICAL TRACERY. (14TH CENTURY.)

When two windows were placed close together it began to be customary to include them under one outer arch, and after a time to pierce the solid head between them with a circle, which frequently was cusped, forming often a quatrefoil (Fig. 17). This completed the idea of a group, and was rapidly followed by ornamental treatment. Three, four, five, or more windows (which in such a position are often termed lights) were often placed under one arch, the head of which was filled by a more or less rich group of circles; mouldings were added, and thus rose the system of decoration for window-heads known as tracery. So long as the tracery preserves the simple character of piercings through a flat stone, filling the space between the window heads, it is known as plate tracery. The thinning down of the blank space to a comparatively narrow surface went on, and by and by the use of mouldings caused that plain surface to resemble bars of stone bent into a circular form: this was called bar tracery, and it is in this form that tracery is chiefly employed in England (Fig. 18). Westminster Abbey is full of exquisite examples of E. E. window-tracery (temp. Henry III.); as, for example, in the windows of the choir, the great circular windows (technically termed rose-windows) at the ends of the transepts, the windows of the chapter-house. Last, but not least, the splendid arcade which forms the triforium is filled with tracery similar in every respect to the best window tracery of the period (Fig. 19).

FIG. 19.—THE TRIFORIUM ARCADE, WESTMINSTER ABBEY.
(1269.)

In the decorated style of the fourteenth century tracery was developed till it reached a great pitch of perfection and intricacy. In the earlier half of the century none save regular geometrical forms, made up of circles and segments of circles, occur; in other words, the whole design of the most elaborate window could be drawn with the compasses, and a curve of contrary flexure rarely occurred. In the latest half of that period flowing lines are introduced into the tracery, and very much alter its character (Fig. 20). The cusping throughout is bolder than in the E. E. period.

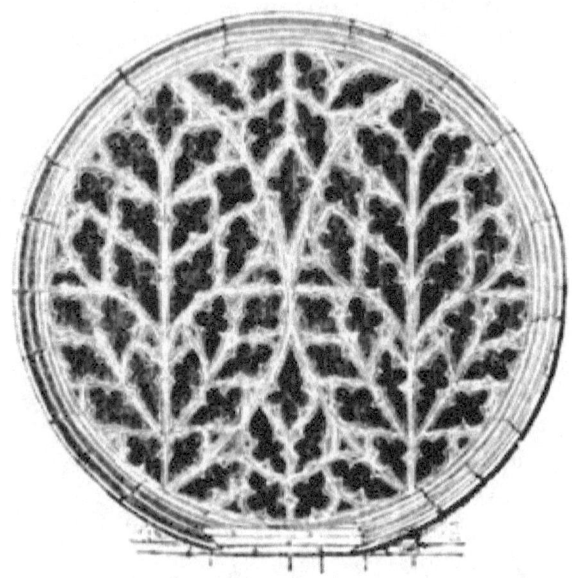

FIG. 20.—ROSE WINDOW FROM THE TRANSEPT OF LINCOLN CATHEDRAL. (1342-1347.)

In perpendicular windows spaces of enormous size are occupied by the mullions and tracery. Horizontal bars, called transoms, are now for the first time introduced, and the upright bars or mullions form with them a kind of stone grating; but below each transom a series of small stone arches forms heads to the lights below that transom, and a minor mullion often springs from the head of each of these arches, so that as the window increases in height, the number of its lights increases. The character of the cusping changed again, the cusps becoming club-headed in their form (Fig. 21).

FIG. 21.—PERPENDICULAR WINDOW.

Arches in the great arcades of churches, or in the smaller arcades of cloisters, or used as decorations to the surface of the walls, were made acute, obtuse, or segmental, to suit the duty they had to perform; but when there was nothing to dictate any special shape, the arch of the E. E. period was by preference acute[20] and of lofty proportions, and that of the Dec. less lofty, and its head equilateral (*i.e.* described so that if the ends of the base of an equilateral triangle touch the two points from which it springs, the apex of the angle shall touch the point of the arch). In the Perp. period the four centred depressed arch, sometimes called the Tudor arch, was introduced, and though it did not entirely supersede the equilateral arch, yet its employment became at last all but universal, and it is one of the especially characteristic features of the Tudor period.

Roofs and Vaults.

The external and the internal covering of a building are very often not the same; the outer covering is then usually called a roof—the other, a vault or ceiling. In not a few Gothic buildings, however, they were the same; such buildings had what are known as open roofs—*i.e.* roofs in which the whole of the timber framing of which they are constructed is open to view from the interior right up to the tiles or lead. Very few open roofs of E. E. character are now remaining, but a good many parish churches retain roofs of the Dec., and more of the Perp. period. The roof of Westminster Hall (Perp., erected 1397) shows how fine an architectural

---

[20] For illustrations consult the Glossary under *Arch*.

object such a roof may become. The roof of the hall of Eltham Palace (Fig. 22) is another good example. Wooden ceilings, often very rich, are not uncommon, especially in the churches of Norfolk and Suffolk, but greater interest attaches to the stone vaults with which the majority of Gothic buildings were erected, than to any other description of covering to the interiors of buildings.

The vault was a feature rarely absent from important churches, and the structural requirements of the Gothic vault were among the most influential of the elements which determined both the plan and the section of a mediæval church. There was a regular growth in Gothic vaults. Those of the thirteenth century are comparatively simple; those of the fourteenth are much richer and more elaborate, and often involve very great structural difficulties. Those of the fifteenth are more systematic, and consequently more simple in principle than the ones which preceded them, but are such marvels of workmanship, and so enriched by an infinity of parts, that they astonish the beholder, and it appears, till the secret is known, impossible to imagine how they can be made to stand.

FIG. 22.—ROOF OF HALL AT ELTHAM PALACE. (15TH CENTURY.)

It has been held by some very good authorities that the pointed arch was first introduced into Gothic architecture to solve difficulties which presented themselves in the vaulting. In all probability the desire to give to everything, arches included, a more lofty appearance and more slender proportions may have had as much to do with the adoption of the pointed arch as any structural considerations, but there can be no doubt that it was used for structural arches from the very first, even when window heads and wall arcades were semicircular, and that the introduction of it cleared the way for the use of stone vaults of large span to a wonderful extent. It is not easy to explain this without being more technical than is perhaps desirable in the present volume, but the subject is one of too much importance for it to be possible to avoid making the attempt.

Churches, it will be recollected, were commonly built with a wide nave and narrower aisles, and it was in the Norman period customary to vault the aisles and cover the nave with a ceiling. There was no difficulty in so spacing the distances apart of the piers of the main arcade that the compartments (usually termed bays) of the aisle should be square on plan; and it was quite possible, without doing more than the Romans had done, to vault each bay of the aisles with a semicircular intersecting vault (*i.e.* one which has the appearance of a semicircular or waggon-head vault, intersected by another vault of the same outline and height). This produced a simple series of what are called groined or cross vaults, which allowed height to be given to the window heads of the aisle and to the arcades between the aisles and nave.

After a time it was desired to vault the nave also, and to adopt for it an intersecting vault, so that the heads of the windows of the clerestory might be raised above the springing line of the vault, but so long as the arches remained semicircular, this was very difficult to accomplish.

The Romans would probably have contented themselves with employing a barrel vault and piercing it to the extent required by short lateral vaults, but the result would have been an irregular, weak, curved line at each intersection with the main vault; and the aisle vaults having made the pleasing effect of a perfectly regular intersection familiar, this expedient does not seem to have found favour, at any rate in England.

Other expedients were however tried, and with curious results. It was for example attempted to vault the nave with a cross vault, embracing two bays of the arcade to one of the vault, but the wall space so gained was particularly ill suited to the clerestory windows, as may be seen by examining the nave of St. Stephen's at Caen. In short, if the vaulting compartment were as wide as the nave one way, but only as wide as the aisle the other way, and semicircular arches alone were employed, a satisfactory result seemed to be unattainable.

In the search for some means of so vaulting a bay of oblong plan that the arches should spring all at one level, and the groins or lines of intersection should cross one another in the centre of the ceiling, the idea either arose or was suggested that the curve of the smaller span should be a pointed instead of a semicircular arch.

The moment this was tried all difficulty vanished, and groined (*i.e.* intersecting) vaults, covering compartments of any proportions became easy to design and simple to construct, for if the vault which spanned the narrow way of the compartment were acutely pointed, and that which spanned it the wide way were either semicircular or flatly-pointed, it became easy to arrange that the startings of both vaults should be at the same level, and that they should rise to the same height, which is the condition essential to the production of a satisfactory intersection.

Scott enumerates not fewer than fourteen varieties of mediæval vaults[21] and points out that specimens of thirteen are to be found at Westminster. Without such minute detail we may select some well-known varieties: — (1) The plain waggon-head vault, as at the Chapel of the Tower; (2) in advanced Norman works, cross-vaults formed by two intersecting semicircular vaults, the diagonal line being called a groin. (3) The earliest transitional and E. E. vaults, pointed and with transverse and diagonal ribs, and bosses at the intersection of ribs, *e.g.*, in the aisles and the early part of the cloisters at Westminster. (4) In the advanced part of the E. E. period, the addition of a rib at the ridge, as seen in the presbytery and transepts at Westminster. (5) At the time of the transition to Dec. (*temp.* Ed. 1.) additional ribs began to be introduced between the diagonal and the transverse ribs. (6) As the Dec. period advanced other ribs, called *liernes*, were introduced, running in various directions over the surface of the vault, making star-like figures on the vault. (7) The vault of the early Perp., which is similar to the last, but more complicated and approaching No. 8, *e.g.*, Abbot Islip's chapel. (8) Lastly, the distinctive vault of the advanced or Tudor Perp., is the fan-tracery vault of which Henry VII.'s Chapel roof is the climax. The vaulting surfaces in these are portions of hollow conoids, and are covered by a net-work of fine ribs, connected together by bands of cusping (Fig. 23).

---

[21] Address to the Conference of Architects. Reported in the *Builder* of 24th June, 1876. Outlines illustrating some of these varieties of vault will be found in the Glossary under *Vault*.

FIG. 23.—HENRY VII.'S CHAPEL. (1503-1512.)

In Scott's enumeration the vaults of octagons and irregular compartments, and such varieties as the one called sexpartite, find a place; here they have been intentionally excluded. Many of them are works of the greatest skill and beauty, especially the vaults of octagonal chapter houses springing from one centre pier (*e.g.*, Chapter Houses at Worcester, Westminster, Wells, and Salisbury).

Externally, the roofs of buildings became very steep in the thirteenth century; they were not quite so steep in the fourteenth, and in the fifteenth they were frequently almost flat. They were always relied upon to add to the effectiveness of a building, and were enriched sometimes by variegated tiles or other covering, sometimes by the introduction of small windows, known as dormer windows, each with its own gablet and its little roof, and sometimes by the addition of a steep sided roof in the shape of a lantern or a "flèche" on the ridge, or a pyramidal covering to some projecting octagon or turret.

All these have their value in breaking up the sky-line of the building, and adding interest and beauty to it. Still more striking, however, in its effect on the sky-line was the spire, a feature to which great attention was paid in English architecture.

Spires.

The early square towers of Romanesque churches were sometimes surmounted by pyramidal roofs of low pitch. We have probably none now remaining, but we have some examples of large pinnacles, crowned with pyramids, which show what the shape must have been. They were square in plan and somewhat steep in slope.

The spire was developed early in the E. E. period. It was octagonal in plan, and the four sides which coincided with the faces of the tower rose direct from the walls above a slightly masked eaves course. The four oblique sides are connected to the tower by a feature called a broach, which may be described as part of a blunt pyramid. The broach-spire (Fig. 24) is to be met with in many parts of England, but especially in Northamptonshire. The chief ornaments of an E. E. spire consist in small windows (called spire-lights or lucarnes) each surmounted by its gablet.

**FIG. 24.—EARLY ENGLISH SPIRE. CHURCH OF ST. MARY MAG-
DALENE, WARBOYS, LINCOLNSHIRE.**

In the Dec. period it was common to finish the tower by a parapet, and to start
the spire behind the parapet, sometimes with a broach, often without. Pinnacles

were frequently added at the corners of the tower, and an arch, like that of a flying buttress, was sometimes thrown across from the pinnacle to the spire. Spire-lights occur as before, and the surface of the spire is often enriched by bands of ornament at intervals. The general proportions of the spire were more slender than before, and the rib, which generally ran up each angle, was often enriched by crockets, *i.e.* tufts of leaves arranged in a formal shape (Fig. 25).

FIG. 25.—DECORATED SPIRE. ALL SAINTS' CHURCH, OAKHAM, RUTLANDSHIRE.

Towers were frequently intended to stand without spires in the Perp. period, and are often finished by four effective angle-pinnacles and a cornice with battlements. Where spires occur in this period they resemble those of the Dec. period.

Spires end usually in a boss or finial, surmounted by a weathercock. Ordinary roofs were usually finished by ornamental cresting, and their summits were marked by finials,[22] frequently of exquisite workmanship.

Ornaments.

We now come to ornaments, including mouldings, carving, and colour, and here we are landed upon a mass of details which it would be impossible to pursue far. Mouldings play a prominent part in Gothic architecture, and from the first to the last they varied so constantly that their profiles and grouping may be constantly made use of as a kind of architectural calendar, to point out the time, to within a few years, when the building in which they occur was erected.

A moulding is the architect's means of drawing a line on his building. If he desires to mark on the exterior the position of an internal floor, or in any other way to suggest a division into storeys, a moulded string-course is introduced. If he wishes to add richness and play of light and shade to the sides of an important arch, he introduces a series of mouldings, the profile of which has been designed to form lights and shadows such as will answer his purpose. If again he desires to throw out a projection and to give the idea of its being properly supported, he places under his projection a corbel of mouldings which are of strong as well as pleasing form, so as to convey to the eye the notion of support. Mouldings, it can be understood, differ in both size and profile, according to the purpose which they are required to serve, the distance from the spectator at which they are fixed, and the material out of which they are formed. In the Gothic periods they also differed according to the date at which they were executed.

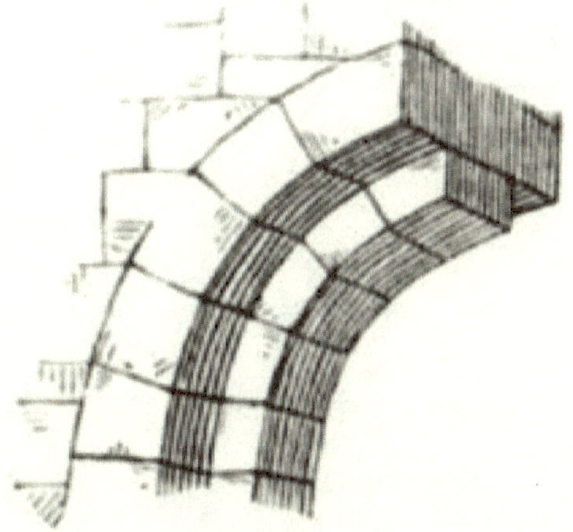

FIG. 26.—EARLY ARCH IN RECEDING PLANES.

---

[22] See Glossary.

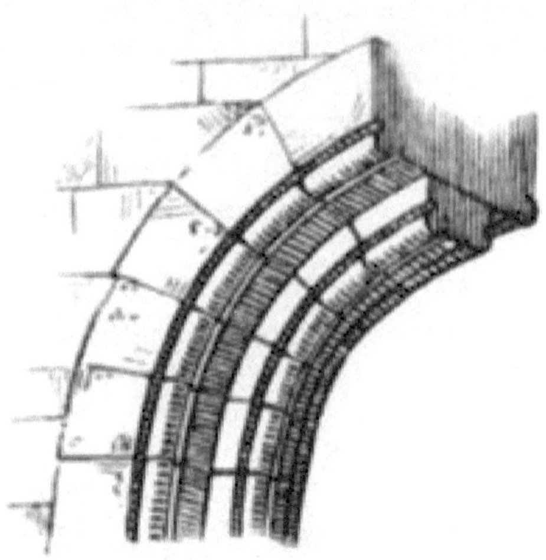

FIG. 27.—ARCH IN RECEDING PLANES MOULDED.

The first step towards the Gothic system of mouldings was taken by the Romanesque architects when the idea of building arches in thick walls, not only one within the others, but also in planes receding back from the face of the wall one behind as well as within another, was formed and carried out, and when a corresponding recessed arrangement of the jamb of the arch was made (Fig. 26). The next step was the addition of some simple moulding to the advancing angle of each rim of such a series of arches either forming a bead (Fig. 27) or a chamfer.

In the transitional part of the twelfth century and the E. E. period this process went on till at last, though the separate receding arches still continued to exist, the mouldings[23] into which they were cut became so numerous and elaborate as to render it often difficult to detect the subordination or division into distinct planes which really remained.

---

[23] For illustrations consult the Glossary.

**FIG. 28.—DOORWAY, KING'S COLLEGE CHAPEL, CAMBRIDGE.
(15TH CENTURY.)**

This passion for elaborate mouldings, often extraordinarily undercut, reached its climax in the thirteenth century, the E. E. period. In the Dec. period, while almost everything else became more elaborate, mouldings grew more simple, yet hardly less beautiful. In the Perp. period they were not only further simplified, but often impoverished, being usually shallow, formal, and stiff.[24]

Ornaments abounded, and included not only enrichments in the shape of carved foliage and figures, statuary, mosaics, and so forth, but ornamental features, such as canopies, pinnacles, arcades, and recesses (Fig. 28).

In each period these are distinct in design from all that went before or came after, and thus to catch the spirit of any one Gothic period aright, it is not enough to fix the general shapes of the arches and proportions of the piers but every fea-

---

[24] For further illustrations see the Glossary.

ture, every moulding, and every ornament must be wrought in the true spirit of the work, or the result will be marred.

Stained Glass.

Ornamental materials and every sort of decorative art, such as mosaic, enamel, metal work and inlays, were freely employed to add beauty in appropriate positions; but there was one ornament, the crowning invention of the Gothic artists, which largely influenced the design of the finest buildings, and which reflected a glory on them such as nothing else can approach: this was stained glass.

So much of the old glass has perished, and so little modern glass is even passable, that this praise may seem overcharged to those who have never seen any of the best specimens still left. We have in the choir at Canterbury a remnant of the finest sort of glass which England possesses. Some good fragments remain at Westminster, though not very many; but to judge of the effect of glass at its best, the student should visit La Sainte Chapelle at Paris, or the Cathedrals of Chartres, Le Mans, Bourges, or Rheims, and he will find in these buildings effects in colour which are nothing less than gorgeous in their brilliancy, richness, and harmony.

FIG. 29.—STAINED GLASS WINDOW FROM CHARTRES CATHE-
DRAL.

The peculiar excellence of stained glass as compared with every other sort of
decoration, is that it is luminous. To some extent fresco-painting may claim a sort
of brightness; mosaic when executed in polished materials possesses brilliancy;
but in stained glass the light which comes streaming in through the window itself
gives radiance, while the quality of the glass determines the colour, and thus we

obtain a glowing, lustre of colour which can only be compared to the beauty of gems. In order properly to fill their place as decorations, stained-glass windows must be something quite different from transparent pictures, and the scenes they represent must not detach themselves too violently from the general ground. The most perfect effect is produced by such windows as those at Canterbury or Chartres (Fig. 29), which recall a cluster of jewels rather than a picture.

Coloured Decoration.

Colour was also freely introduced by the lavish employment of coloured materials where they were to be had, and by painting the interiors with bright pigments. We meet with traces of rich colour on many parts of ancient buildings, where we should hardly dare to put it now, and we cannot doubt that painted decoration was constantly made use of with the happiest effect.

Sculpture.

FIG. 30.—SCULPTURE FROM THE ENTRANCE TO THE CHAPTER HOUSE, WESTMINSTER ABBEY. (1250.)

The last, perhaps the noblest ornament, is sculpture. The Gothic architects were alive to its value, and in all their best works statues abounded; often conventional to the last degree; sometimes to our eyes uncouth, but always the best which those who carved them could do at the time; always sure to contribute to architectural effect; never without a picturesque power, sometimes rising to grace and even grandeur, and sometimes sinking to grotesque ugliness. Whatever the quality of the sculpture was, it was always there, and added life to the whole. Monsters gaped and grinned from the water-spouts, little figures or strange animals twisted in and out of the foliage at angles and bosses and corbels. Stately effigies occupied dignified niches, in places of honour; and in the mouldings and tympanum of the head of a doorway there was often carved a whole host of figures representing heaven, earth, and hell, with a rude force and a native eloquence that have not lost their power to the present day.

In the positions where modest ornamentation was required, as for example the capitals of shafts, the hollows of groups of mouldings, and the bosses of vaulting, carving of the most finished execution and masterly design constantly occurs. Speaking roughly, this was chiefly conventional in the E. E. period, chiefly natural in the Dec. and mixed, but with perhaps a preference for the conventional in the Perp. Examples abound, but both for beauty and accessibility we can refer to no better example than the carving which enriches the entrance to the Chapter House of Westminster Abbey (Fig. 30).

MISERERE SEAT FROM WELLS CATHEDRAL.

CHAPTER VI.

GOTHIC ARCHITECTURE IN WESTERN EUROPE.

FRANCE.—CHRONOLOGICAL SKETCH.

1. France. Chronological Sketch. Analysis of Buildings. Plans. Walls, Towers and Gables. Columns and Piers. Roofs and Vaults. Openings. Mouldings and Ornaments. Construction and Design

THE architecture of France during the Middle Ages throws much light upon the history of the country. The features in which it differs from the work done in England at the same period can, many of them, be directly traced to differences in the social, political, or religious situation of the two nations at the time. For example, we find England in the eleventh and twelfth centuries in the hands of the Normans, a newly-conquered country under uniform administration; and accordingly few local variations occur in the architecture of our Norman period. The twelfth-century work, at Durham or Peterborough for instance, differs but little from that at Gloucester or Winchester. In France the case is different. That country was divided into a series of semi-independent provinces, whose inhabitants differed, not only in the leaders whom they followed, but in speech, race, and customs. As might be expected, the buildings of each province presented an aspect different in many respects from those of every other; and we may as well add that these peculiarities did not die out with the end of the round-arched period of architecture, but lingered far into the pointed period.

FIG. 31.—CHURCH AT FONTEVRAULT. (BEGUN 1125.)

The south of France was occupied by people speaking what are now known as the Romance dialects, and some writers have adopted the name as descriptive of the peculiarities of the architecture of these districts. The Romance provinces clung tenaciously to their early forms of art, so that pointed architecture was not established in the south of France till half a century, and in some places nearly a whole century, later than in the north.

On the other hand, the Frankish part of the country was the cradle of Gothic. The transition from round to pointed architecture first took place in the royal domain, of which Paris was the centre, and it may be assumed that the new style was already existing when in 1140 Abbot Suger laid the foundations of the choir of the church of St. Denis, about forty years before the commencement of the eastern arm of our own Canterbury.

De Caumont, who in his "Abécédaire" did for French architecture somewhat the same work of analysis and scientific arrangement which Rickman performed for English, has adopted the following classification:—

Romanesque Architecture. *Architecture Romane.*	Primitive. *Primordiale.*	5th to 10th century.
	Second. *Secondaire.*	End of 10th to commencement of 12th century.
	Third or Transition *Tertiaire ou de Transition.*	12th century.
Pointed Architecture. *Architecture ogivale.*	First. *Primitive.*	13th century.
	Second. *Secondaire.*	14th century.
	Third. *Tertiaire.*	15th century.

FIG. 32.—DOORWAY AT LOCHES, FRANCE. (1180.)

The transitional architecture of France is no exception to the rule that the art of a period of change is full of interest. Much of it has disappeared, but examples remain in the eastern part of the cathedral of St. Denis already referred to, in portions of the cathedrals of Noyon and Sens, the west front of Chartres, the church of St. Germain des Prés at Paris, and elsewhere. We here often find the pointed arch employed for the most important parts of the structure, while the round arch is still retained in the window and door-heads, and in decorative arcades, as shown in our illustrations of a section of the church at Fontevrault (Fig. 31), and of a doorway at Loches (Fig. 32).

The first pointed architecture of the thirteenth century in France differs considerably from the early English of this country. The arches are usually less acute, and the windows not so tall in proportion to their width. The mouldings employed are few and simple compared with the many and intricate English ones. Large round columns are much used in place of our complicated groups of small shafts for the piers of the nave; and the abacus of the capital remains square. An air of breadth and dignity prevails in the buildings of this date to which the simple details, noble proportions, and great size largely contribute. The western front of Notre Dame, Paris (Fig. 33), dates from the early years of this century, the interior being much of it a little earlier. The well-known cathedrals of Chartres, Rheims, Laon, and later in the style, Amiens, and Beauvais, may be taken as grand examples of French first pointed. To these may be added the very graceful Sainte Chapelle of Paris, the choir and part of the nave of the cathedral at Rouen, the church of St. Etienne at Caen, and the cathedrals of Coutances, Lisieux, Le Mans, and Bourges. This list of churches could be almost indefinitely extended, and many monastic buildings, and not a few domestic and military ones, might be added. Among the most conspicuous of these may be named the monastic fortress at Mont St. Michel, probably the most picturesque structure in France, the remarkable fortifications of Carcassonne, and the lordly castle of Coucy.

FIG. 33.—NOTRE DAME, PARIS, WEST FRONT. (1214.)

The second pointed, or fourteenth century Gothic of France, bears more resemblance to contemporary English Gothic than the work of the centuries preceding or following. Large windows for stained glass, with rich geometrical tracery prevailed, and much the same sort of ornamental treatment as in England was adopted in richly decorated buildings. Specimens of the work of this century occur everywhere in the shape of additions to the great churches and cathedrals which had been left unfinished from the previous century, and also of side chapels which it became customary to add to the aisles of churches. The great and well-known abbey of St. Ouen at Rouen is one of the few first-class churches which can be named as begun and almost entirely completed in this century. The tower and spire of the church of St. Pierre at Caen (Fig. 13) are very well-known and beautiful specimens of this period.

French fifteenth century architecture, or third pointed, is far from being so dignified or so scientific as English perpendicular, and differs from it considerably. Exuberant richness in decoration was the rage, and shows itself both in sculpture, tracery, and general design. Much of the later work of this period has received the name of flamboyant, because of the flame-like shapes into which the tracery of the heads of windows was thrown. In flamboyant buildings we often meet with art which, though certainly over-florid, is brilliant, rich, and full of true feeling for decoration.

In this century, secular and domestic buildings attained more prominence than at any previous periods. Some of them are among the best works which this period produced. Familiar examples will be found in the noble Palais de Justice at Rouen, and the Hôtel de Bourgtherould in the same city; in parts of the great château at Blois, the splendid château of Pierrefonds, and the Hôtels de Ville of Oudenarde and Caen.

FRANCE.—ANALYSIS OF BUILDINGS.

Plan.

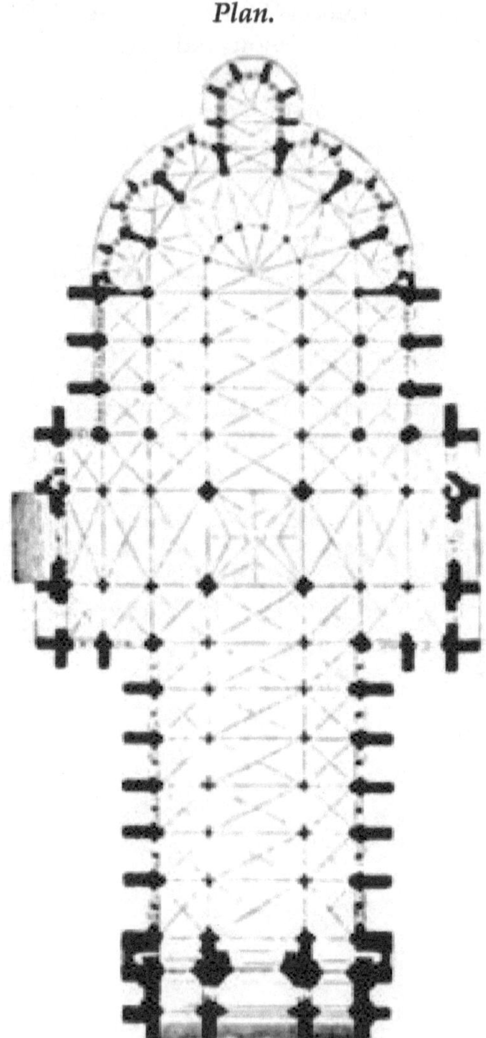

FIG. 34.—PLAN OF AMIENS CATHEDRAL. (1220-1272.)

The plans of French cathedrals and other buildings conform in general to the description of Gothic plans given in Chapter II., but they have of course certain distinctive peculiarities (Fig. 34). The cathedrals are as a rule much broader in proportion to their length than English ones. Double aisles frequently occur, and not infrequently an added range of side chapels fringes each of the main side walls, so that the interior of one of these vast buildings presents, in addition to the main vista along the nave, many delightful cross views of great extent. The transepts are also much less strongly marked than our English examples. There are even some great cathedrals (*e.g.*, Bourges) without transepts; and where they exist it is common to find that, as in the case of Notre Dame de Paris, they do not project beyond the line of the side walls, so that, although fairly well-marked in the exterior and interior of the building, they add nothing to its floor-space. The eastern end of a French cathedral (and indeed of French churches generally, with very few exceptions) is terminated in an apse. When, as is frequently the case, this apse is encircled by a ring of chapels, with flying buttresses on several stages rising from among them, the whole arrangement is called a *chevet*, and very striking and busy is the appearance which it presents.

Walls, Towers, and Gables.

The walls are rarely built of any other material than stone, and much splendid masonry is to be found in France. Low towers are often to be met with, and so are projecting staircase turrets of polygonal or circular forms. The façades of cathedrals, including ends of transepts as well as west fronts, are most striking, and often magnificently enriched. It is an interesting study to examine a series of these fronts, each a little more advanced than the last, as for example Notre Dame (Fig. 33), the transept at Rouen, Amiens (Fig. 35), and Rheims, and to note how the horizontal bands and other level features grow less and less conspicuous, while the vertical ones are more and more strongly marked; showing an increasing desire, not only to make the buildings lofty, but to suppress everything which might interfere with their looking as high as possible.

FIG. 35.—AMIENS CATHEDRAL, WEST FRONT. (1220-1272.)

Columns and Piers.

The column is a greater favourite than the pier in France, as has already been said. Sometimes, where the supports of the main arcade are really piers, they are built like circular shafts of large size; and even when they have no capital (as was the case in third-pointed examples), these piers still retain much of the air of solid strength which belongs to the column, and which the French architects appear to have valued highly. In cases where a series of mouldings has to be carried—as for example when the main arcade of a building is richly moulded—English architects would usually have provided a distinct shaft for each little group (or as Willis named them order), into which the whole can be subdivided. In France, at any rate during the earlier periods, the whole series of mouldings would spring from the square unbroken abacus of a single large column, to which perhaps one shaft, or as in our illustration (Fig. 36) four shafts, would be attached which would be carried up to the springing of the nave vault, at which point the same treatment would be repeated, though on a smaller scale, with the moulded ribs of that vault.

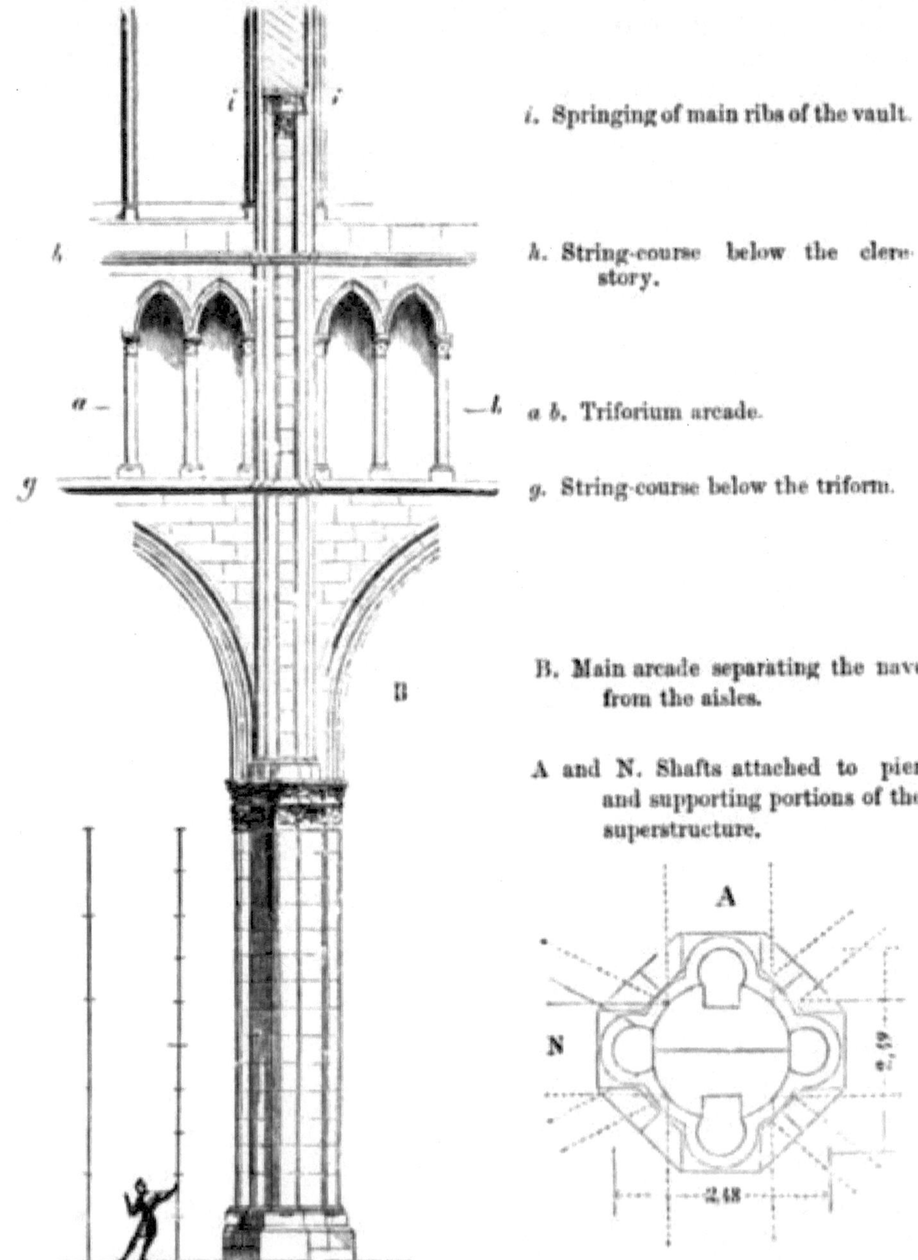

FIG. 36.—PIERS AND SUPERSTRUCTURE, RHEIMS CATHEDRAL.
(1211-1240.)

A peculiarity of some districts of southern France is the suppression of the external buttress; the buttresses are in fact built within the church walls instead of outside, and masonry enough is added to make each into a separating wall which divides side chapels. Some large churches, *e.g.*, the cathedral at Alby, in Southern France, consist of a wide nave buttressed in this way, and having side chapels between the buttresses, but without side aisles.

The plans of the secular, military, and domestic buildings of France also present many interesting peculiarities, but not such as it is possible to review within the narrow limits of this chapter.

Roofs and Vaults.

The peculiarly English feature of an open roof is hardly ever met with in any shape: yet though stone vaults are almost universal, they are rarely equal in scientific skill to the best of those in our own country. In transitional examples, many very singular instances of the expedients employed before the pointed vault was fully developed can be found. In some of the central and southern districts, domes, or at least domical vaults, were employed. (See the section of Fontevrault, Fig. 31). The dome came in from Byzantium. It was introduced in Perigord, where the very curious and remarkable church of St. Front (begun early in the eleventh century) was built. This is to all intents a Byzantine church. It is an almost exact copy in plan and construction of St. Mark's at Venice, a church designed and built by Eastern architects, and it is roofed by a series of domes, a peculiarity which is as distinctive of Byzantine (*i.e.*, Eastern early Christian), as the vaulted roof is of Romanesque (or Western early Christian) architecture. Artists from Constantinople itself probably visited France, and from this centre a not inconsiderable influence extended itself in various directions, and led to the use of many Byzantine features both of design and ornament.

As features in the exterior of their buildings, the roofs have been in every period valued by the French architects; they are almost always steep, striking, and ornamented. All appropriate modes of giving prominence and adding ornament to a roof have been very fully developed in French Gothic architecture, and the roofs of semicircular and circular apses, staircase towers, &c., may be almost looked upon as typical.[25]

Openings.

The treatment of openings gives occasion for one of the most strongly marked points of contrast between French and English Gothic architecture. With us the great windows are unquestionably the prominent features, but with the French the doors are most elaborated. This result is reached not so much by any lowering of the quality of the treatment bestowed upon the windows, but by the greatly increased importance given to doorways.

The great portals of Notre Dame at Paris (Fig. 33), Rheims, or Amiens (Fig. 35), and the grand porches of Chartres may be named as the finest examples, and are probably the most magnificent single features which Gothic Art produced in any age or any country; but in its degree the western portal of every great church is usually an object upon which the best resources of the architect have been free-

[25] For an example of these see the house of Jaques Cœur (Fig. 7).

ly lavished. The wall is built very thick so that enormous jambs, carrying a vast moulded arch, can be employed. The head of the door is filled with sculpture, which is also lavishly used in the sides and arch, and over the whole rises an ornamental gable, frequently profusely adorned with tracery and sculpture, its sides being richly decorated by crockets or similar ornaments, and crowned by a sculptured terminal or finial.

The windows in the earliest periods are simpler than in our E. E., as well as of less slender proportions. In the second and third periods they are full of rich tracery, and are made lofty and wide to receive the magnificent stained glass with which it was intended to fill them, and which many churches retain. Circular windows, sometimes called wheel-windows, often occupy the gables, and are many of them very fine compositions.

Mouldings and Ornaments.

The mouldings of the French first pointed are usually larger than our own. Compared with ours they are also fewer, simpler, and designed to produce more breadth of effect. This may partly result from their originating in a sunshiny country where effects of shade are easily obtained. In the second and third periods they more nearly resemble those in use in England at the corresponding times.

The carving is very characteristic and very beautiful. In the transition and first pointed a cluster of stalks, ending in a tuft of foliage or flowers, is constantly employed, especially in capitals. The use of this in England is rare; and, on the other hand, foliage like E. E. conventional foliage is rare in France. In the second pointed, natural foliage is admirably rendered (Fig. 37). In the third a somewhat conventional kind of foliage, very luxuriant in its apparent growth, is constantly met with.

This carving is at every stage accompanied by figure-sculpture of the finest character. Heads of animals, statues, groups of figures, and has reliefs are freely employed, but always with the greatest judgment, so that their introduction adds richness to the very point in the whole composition where it is most needed. In every part of France, and in every period of Gothic architecture, good specimens of sculpture abound. Easily accessible illustrations will be found in the west entrance and south transept front of Rouen Cathedral, the porches and portals at Chartres, the choir inclosure of Notre Dame at Paris, and the richly sculptured inclosure of the choir of Amiens Cathedral.

FIG. 37.—CAPITAL FROM ST. NICHOLAS, BLOIS, FRANCE. (13TH CENTURY.)

Stained glass has been more than once referred to. It is to be found in its greatest perfection in France, as for example in La Sainte Chapelle at Paris, and the cathedrals of Le Mans, Bourges, Chartres, and Rheims. All that has been said in the introductory chapter on this, the crowning ornament of Gothic architecture, and on its influence upon window design, and through that, upon the whole structure of the best churches, is to the full as applicable to French examples. Coloured decoration was also frequently employed in the interior of churches and other buildings, and is constantly to be met with in French buildings, both secular and religious. In most cases, however, it is less easy to appreciate this than the stained glass, for, as it is now to be seen, the colours are either faded and darkened by time and smoke, or else restored, not always with the exactness that could be desired.

Construction and Design.

The construction of the great buildings of the middle ages in France is an interesting subject of study, but necessarily a thoroughly technical one. Great sagacity in designing the masonry, carpentry, joinery, and metal-work; and trained skill in the carrying out the designs, have left their traces everywhere; and while the construction of the earlier castles and of the simple churches shows a solidity but little inferior to that of the Romans themselves, the most elaborate works, such for example as the choir at Beauvais (Fig. 38), can hardly be surpassed as specimens of skill and daring, careful forethought, and bold execution.

FIG. 38.—BEAUVAIS CATHEDRAL, INTERIOR. (1225-1537.)

Design, in France, pursued the general principles of Gothic architecture to their logical conclusions with the most uncompromising consistency. Perhaps the most distinctive peculiarity in French cathedrals is a love of abstract beauty, and a strong preference for breadth, regularity, dignity, and symmetry wherever they come into competition with picturesqueness and irregular grouping. There is, it is true, plenty of the picturesque element in French mediæval art; but if we take the finest buildings, and those in which the greatest effort would be made to secure the qualities which were considered the greatest and most desirable, we shall find very strong evidences of a conviction that beauty was to be attained by regularity and order, rather than by unsymmetrical and irregular treatment.

BELGIUM AND THE NETHERLANDS.

2. Belgium and the Netherlands

Belgium is a country rich in remains of Gothic architecture. Its art was influenced so largely by its neighbourhood to France, that it will not be necessary to attempt anything like a chronological arrangement of its buildings. Fine churches exist in its principal cities, but they cannot be said to form a series differing widely from the churches of France, with which they were contemporary, and where they differ the advantage is generally on the side of the French originals.

The principal cathedral of the Low Countries, that at Antwerp, is a building remarkable for its great width (having seven aisles), and for the wonderful picturesqueness of its interior. The exterior, which is unfinished, is also very effective, with its one lofty spire. The other cathedrals of note include those of Tournay, Brussels, Mechlin, Louvain, Liége, and Ghent. Belgium also possesses a great number of large parochial churches.

When we turn to secular buildings we find the Belgian architecture of the middle ages taking a leading position. The free cities of Belgium acquired municipal privileges at an early date, and accumulated great wealth. Accordingly we find town halls, trade halls, belfries, warehouses, and excellent private dwelling-houses in abundance. The cloth hall at Ypres has been repeatedly illustrated and referred to as an example of a grand and effective building for trade purposes; it is of thirteenth-century architecture and of great size, its centre marked by a massive lofty tower; and its angles carrying slight turrets; but in other respects it depends for its effectiveness solely on its repetition of similar features. Examples of the same kind of architecture exist at Louvain and Ghent.

The Town Halls of Brussels, Louvain, Bruges, Mechlin, Ghent, Oudenarde, and Ypres, are all buildings claiming attention. They were most of them in progress during the fifteenth century, and are fine, but florid examples of late Gothic. Some one or two at least of the town halls were begun and partly carried out in the fourteenth century; on the other hand, the Hôtel de Ville at Oudenarde, was begun as late as the beginning of the sixteenth; so were the Exchange at Antwerp (destroyed by fire and rebuilt not long since) and some other well-known structures: their architecture, though certainly Gothic, is debased in style.

The general aspect of these famous buildings was noble and bold in mass, and rich in ornament. Our illustration (Fig. 39) shows the Town Hall of Middleburgh in Holland; one which is less famous and of smaller dimensions than those enumerated above, but equally characteristic.

The main building usually consisted of a long unbroken block surmounted by a high-pitched roof, and usually occupied one side of a public place. The side of the building presents several storeys, filled by rows of fine windows, though in some cases the lowest storey is occupied by an open arcade. The steep roof, usually crowded with dormer windows, carries up the eye to a lofty ridge, and from the centre of it rises the lofty tower which forms so conspicuous a feature in most of these buildings. In the Town Hall at Bruges the tower is comparatively simple, though of a mass and height that are truly imposing; but in Brussels, Ypres, and other examples, it is a richly ornamented composition on which every resource of the mason and the carver has been lavished. Our illustration (Fig. 40) shows the well-known tower at Ghent.

FIG. 39.—THE TOWN HALL OF MIDDLEBURGH. (1518.)

FIG. 40.—TOWER AT GHENT. (BEGUN 1183.)

The gable ends of the great roof are often adorned by pinnacles and other ornaments; but they rarely come prominently into view, as it is invariably the long side of the building which is considered to be the principal front.

SCOTLAND, WALES, AND IRELAND.

3. Scotland, Wales, and Ireland

In Scotland good but simple examples of early work (transition from Romanesque to E. E.) occur, as for example, at Jedburgh and Kelso, Dryburgh and Leuchars abbey churches. A very interesting and in many respects unique cathedral of the thirteenth century, with later additions, exists at Glasgow. It is a building of much beauty, with good tracery, and the crypt offers a perfect study of various and often graceful modes of forming groined vaults. The Cathedral of Elgin (thirteenth century), an admirable Edwardian building, now in ruins, and the Abbey at Melrose, also ruined, of fourteenth century architecture (begun 1322), are both excellent specimens of the art of the periods to which they belong, and bear a close resemblance to what was being done in England at the same time. The famous tower of St. Giles's Cathedral, Edinburgh, and the Chapel at Roslyn, of the fifteenth century, on the other hand, are of thoroughly un-English character, resembling in this respect much of the Scotch architecture of the succeeding centuries; Roslyn is ascribed by Mr. Fergusson to a Spanish or Portuguese architect, with great probability.

Other abbey churches and remains of architectural work exist at Dumblane, Arbroath, Dunkeld, and in many other localities; and Holyrood Palace, still retains part of its elegant early fourteenth-century chapel.

Of secular and domestic work Linlithgow is a fair specimen, but of late date. Most of the castles and castellated mansions of Scotland belong indeed to a later time than the Gothic period, though there is a strong infusion of Gothic feeling in the very picturesque style in which they are designed.

Wales is distinguished for the splendid series of castles to which allusion has been made in a previous chapter. They were erected at the best time of English Gothic architecture (Edward I.) under English direction, and are finely designed and solidly built. Wales can also boast the interesting Cathedrals of Chester, Llandaff, St. David's, and some smaller churches, but in every case there is little to distinguish them from contemporary English work.

Ireland is more remarkable for antiquities of a date anterior to the beginning of the Gothic period than for works belonging to it. A certain amount of graceful and simple domestic work, however, exists there; and in addition to the cathedrals of Kildare, Cashel, and Dublin, numerous monastic buildings, not as a rule large or ambitious, but often graceful and picturesque, are scattered about.

MISERERE SEAT IN WELLS CATHEDRAL.

CHAPTER VII.

GOTHIC ARCHITECTURE IN CENTRAL AND NORTHERN EUROPE.

GERMANY.—CHRONOLOGICAL SKETCH.

1. Germany. Chronological Sketch. Analysis of Buildings. Plans. Walls, Towers and Gables. Roofs and Vaults. Openings. Ornaments. Construction and Design

THE architecture of Germany, from the twelfth to the sixteenth centuries, can be divided into an early, a middle, and a late period, with tolerable distinctness. Of these, the early period possesses the greatest interest, and the peculiarities of its buildings are the most marked and most beautiful. In the middle period, German Gothic bore a very close general resemblance to the Gothic of the same time in France; and, as a rule, such points of difference as exist are not in favour of the German work. Late Gothic work in Germany is very fantastic and unattractive.

**FIG. 41.—ABBEY CHURCH OF ARNSTEIN. (12TH AND 13TH CEN-
TURIES.)**

Through the twelfth, and part of the thirteenth centuries, the architects of Germany pursued a course parallel with that followed in France and in England, but without adopting the pointed arch. They developed the simple and rude Romanesque architecture which prevailed throughout Europe in the tenth and eleventh centuries, and which they learnt originally from Byzantine artists who fled from their own country during the reign of the iconoclasts; and they not only carried it to a point of elaboration which was abreast of the art of our best Norman architecture, but went on further in the same course; for while the French and ourselves were adopting lancet windows and pointed arches, they continued to employ the round-headed window and the semicircular arch in buildings which in their size, richness, loftiness, and general style, correspond with early Gothic examples in other countries. This early German architecture has been sometimes called fully developed Romanesque, and sometimes round-arched Gothic, and both terms may be applied to it without impropriety, for it partakes of the qualities implied by each. The Church of the Holy Apostles at Cologne, and those of St. Martin and St. Maria in Capitolo, in the same city, may be referred to as among the best works of this class. Each of these has an eastern apse, and also an apsidal termination to each transept. The Apostles' church has a low octagon at the crossing, and its sky-line is further broken up by western and eastern towers, the latter of comparatively small size and octagonal; and under the eaves of the roof occurs an arcade of small arches.

A view of the Abbey Church of Arnstein (Fig. 41) illustrates some of the features of these transitional churches. It will be noticed that though there is no transept, there are no less than four towers, two octagonal, and two square, and that the apse is a strongly developed feature.

In the church at Andernach, of which we give an illustration (Fig. 42), the same arrangement, namely, that of four towers, two to the west, and two to the east, may be noticed; but there is not the same degree of difference between the towers, and the result is less happy. This example, like the last, has no central feature, and in both the arcade under the eaves of the roof is conspicuous only by its absence. It does, however, occur on the western towers at Andernach.

FIG. 42.—CHURCH AT ANDERNACH. (EARLY 13TH CENTURY.)

The pointed arch, when adopted in Germany, was in all probability borrowed from France, as the general aspect of German churches of pointed architecture seems to prove. The greatest Gothic cathedral of Germany, Cologne Cathedral, was not commenced till about the year 1275, and its choir was probably completed during the first quarter of the fourteenth century. This cathedral, one of the largest

in Europe, is also one of the grandest efforts of mediæval architecture, and it closely resembles French examples of the same period, both in its general treatment,
and in the detail of its features. The plan of Cologne Cathedral (Fig. 46) is one of the
most regular and symmetrical which has come down to us from the middle ages.
The works were carried on slowly after the choir was consecrated, but without
any deviation from the original plan, though some alteration in style and details
crept in. In our own day the works have been resumed and vigorously pushed on
towards completion; and, the original drawings having been preserved, the two
western towers, the front, and other portions have been carried on in accordance
with them. Cologne, accordingly, presents the almost unique spectacle of a great
Gothic church, erected without deviation from its original plan, and completed
in the style in which it was begun. It is fair to add that though splendid in the extreme, this cathedral has far less charm, and less of that peculiar quality of mystery
and vitality than many, we might say most, of the great cathedrals of Europe.

The plan consists of a nave of eight bays, two of which form a kind of vestibule, and five avenues, *i.e.* two aisles on each side; transepts of four bays each,
with single aisles; and a choir of four bays and an apse, the double aisle of the nave
being continued and carried down the choir. That part of the outer aisle which
sweeps round the apse has been formed into a series of seven polygonal chapels,
thus gaining a complete *chevet*.[26] Over the crossing there is a comparatively slender spire, and at the west end stand two massive towers terminated by a pair of
lofty and elaborate spires, of open tracery, and enriched by crockets, finials, and
much ornamentation. The cathedral is built of stone, without much variation in
colour; it is vaulted throughout, and a forest of flying buttresses surrounds it on all
sides. The beauty of the tracery, the magnificent boldness of the scale of the whole
building, and its orderly regularity, are very imposing, and give it a high rank
among the greatest works of European architecture; but it is almost too majestic
to be lovely, and somewhat cold and uninteresting from its uniform colour, and
perhaps from its great regularity.

Strasburg Cathedral—not so large as Cologne—has been built at various
times; the nave and west front are the work of the best Gothic period. This building has a nave and single aisles, short transepts, and a short apsidal choir. There is
great richness in much of the work; double tracery, *i.e.* a second layer, so to speak,
of tracery, is here employed in the windows, and extended beyond them, but the
effect is not happy. The front was designed to receive two open tracery spires, but
only one of them has been erected. It is amazingly intricate and rich, the workmanship is very astonishing, but the artistic effect is not half so good as that of many
plain stone spires.

Another important German church famous for an open spire is the cathedral
at Friburg. Here only one tower, standing at the middle of the west front, was ever
intended, and partly because the composition is complete as proposed, and partly
because the design of the tracery in the spire itself is more telling, this building
forms a more effective object than Strasburg, though by no means so lofty or so
grandiose.

---

[26] See p. 77 for an explanation of *chevet*.

FIG. 43.—CHURCH OF ST. BARBARA AT KUTTENBERG. EAST END. (1358-1548.)

The Cathedral of St. Stephen at Vienna is a large and exceedingly rich church. In this building the side aisles are carried to almost the same height as the centre avenue—an arrangement not infrequent in German churches having little save novelty to recommend it, and by which the triforium, and, as a rule, the clerestory disappear, and the church is lighted solely by large side windows. The three avenues are covered by one wide roof, which makes a vast and rather clumsy display externally. A lofty tower, surmounted by a fine and elaborate spire of open tracery, stands on one side of the church—an unusual position—and an unfinished companion tower is begun on the corresponding side. Great churches and cathedrals are to be found in many of the cities of Germany, but their salient points are, as a rule, similar to those of the examples which have been already described.

The incomplete Church of St. Barbara at Kuttenberg, in Bohemia, is one of somewhat exceptional design. It has double aisles, but the side walls for the greater part of the length of the church rest upon the arcade dividing the two aisles, instead of that separating the centre avenue from the side one; and a vault over the inner side aisle forms in effect a kind of balcony or gallery in the nave. The illustration (Fig. 43) which we give of the exterior does not of course indicate this peculiarity, but it shows a very good example of a German adaptation of the French *chevet*, and may be considered as a specimen of German pointed architecture at its ripest stage. The church is vaulted, as might be inferred from the forest of flying buttresses; and the vaulting displays some resemblance to our English fan-vaulting in general idea.

German churches include some specimens of unusual disposition or form, as for example the Church of St. Gereon at Cologne, with an oval choir, and one or two double churches, one of the most curious being the one at Schwartz-Rheindorff, of which we give a section and view. (Figs. 44, 45.)

In their doorways and porches the German architects are often very happy. Our illustration (Fig. 47) of one of the portals of the church at Thann may be taken as giving a good idea of the amount of rich ornament often concentrated here: it displays a wealth of decorative sculpture, which was one of the great merits of the German architects.

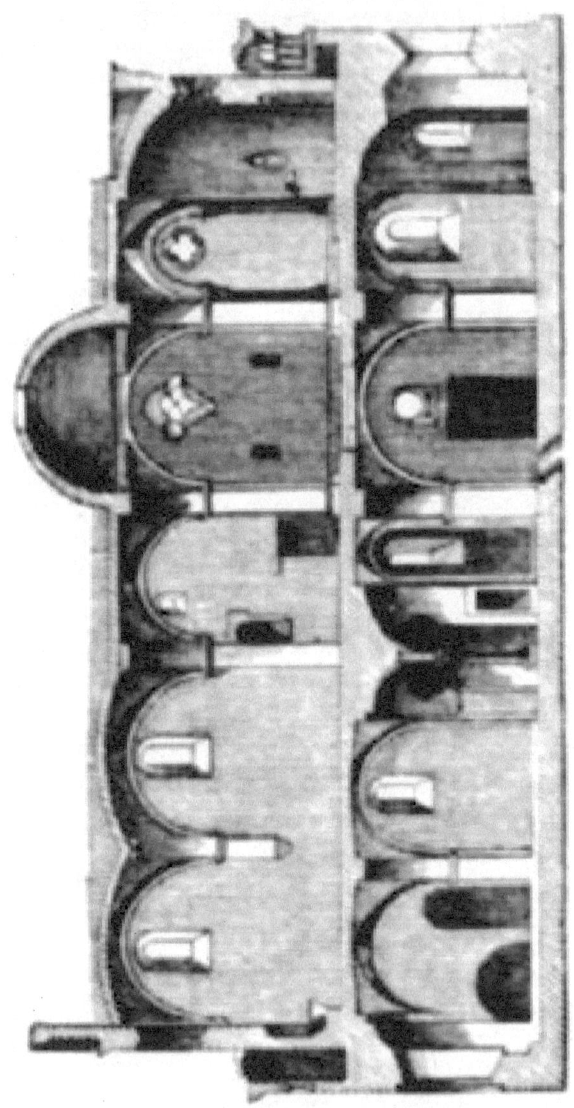

FIG. 44.—DOUBLE CHURCH AT SCHWARTZ-RHEINDORFF. SEC-
TION. (1158.)

The latest development of Gothic in Germany, of which the Church of St.
Catherine at Oppenheim (Fig. 48) is a specimen, was marked (just as late French
was by flamboyant tracery, and late English by fan-vaulting) by a peculiarity in
the treatment of mouldings by which they were robbed of almost all their grace
and beauty, while the execution of them became a kind of masonic puzzle. Two or
more groups of mouldings were supposed to coexist in the same stone, and sometimes a part of one group, sometimes a part of the other group, became visible at
the surface. The name given to this eccentric development is interpenetration.

FIG. 45.—DOUBLE CHURCH AT SCHWARTZ-RHEINDORFF. (A.D. 1158.)

Secular architecture in Germany, though not carried to such a pitch of perfection as in Belgium, was by no means overlooked; but the examples are not numerous. In some of the older cities, such as Prague, Nuremberg, and Frankfort, much picturesque domestic architecture abounds, most of it of the fifteenth and sixteenth centuries, and even later, and all full of piquancy and beauty. In North

Germany, where there is a large tract of country in which building stone is scarce, a style of brick architecture was developed, which was applied to all sorts of purposes with great success. The most remarkable of these brick buildings are the large dwelling-houses, with façades ornamented by brick tracery and panelling, to be found in Eastern Prussia, together with some town halls and similar buildings.

GERMANY.—ANALYSIS OF BUILDINGS.

Plan.

The points of difference between German and French Gothic are not so numerous as to render a very minute analysis of the Gothic of Germany requisite in order to make them clear.

The plans of German churches usually show internal piers; and columns occur but rarely. The churches have nave and aisles, transepts and apsidal choir; but they are peculiar from the frequent use of apses at the ends of the transepts, and also from the occurrence, in not a few instances, of an apse at the west end of the nave as well as at the east end of the choir. They are almost invariably vaulted.

As the style advanced, large churches were constantly planned with double aisles, and the western apse disappeared. Some German church plans, notably those of Cologne Cathedral (Fig. 46) and the great church of St. Lawrence at Nuremberg, are fine specimens of regularity of disposition, though full of many parts.

FIG. 46.—COLOGNE CATHEDRAL. GROUND PLAN. (BEGUN 1248.)

Walls, Towers, and Gables.

The German architects delighted in towers with pointed roofs, and in a multiplicity of them. A highly characteristic feature is a tower of great mass, but often extremely low, covering the crossing. The Cathedral at Mayence shows a fine example of this feature, which was often not more than a low octagon. Western towers, square on plan, are common, and small towers, frequently octagonal, are often employed to flank the choir or in combination with the transepts. These in early examples, are always surmounted by high roofs; in late ones, by stone spires, often of rich open tracery. A very characteristic feature of the round arched Gothic churches is an arcade of small arches immediately below the eaves of the roof and opening into the space above the vaults (Fig. 45). This is rarely wanting in churches built previous to the time when the French type was followed implicitly.

The gables are seldom such fine compositions as in France, or even in Italy; but in domestic and secular buildings many striking gabled fronts occur, the gable being often stepped in outline and full of windows.

Roofs and Vaults.

Vaults are universal in the great churches, and German vaulting has some special peculiarities, but they are such as hardly come within the scope of this handbook. Roofs, however, are so conspicuous that in any general account of German architecture attention must be paid to them. They were from very early times steep in pitch and picturesque in outline, and are evidently much relied upon as giving play to the sky-line. Indeed, for variety of form and piquancy of detail the German roofs are the most successful of the middle ages. The spires, as will have been easily gathered from the descriptions of those at Strasburg, Cologne, &c., became extremely elaborate, and were constructed in many cases entirely of open tracery.

FIG. 47.—WESTERN DOORWAY OF CHURCH AT THANN. (14TH CENTURY.)

FIG. 48.—CHURCH OF ST. CATHERINE AT OPPENHEIM. (1262 TO 1439.)

Openings.

Openings are, on the whole, treated very much as the French treated them. A good example is the western doorway at Thann (Fig. 47); but the use of double tracery in the windows in late examples is characteristic. Sometimes a partial screen of outside tracery is employed in other features besides windows, as may be seen by the very elegant doorway of St. Sebald's Church at Nuremberg, which we have illustrated (Fig. 49).

Ornaments.

The ornaments of German Gothic are often profuse, but rarely quite happy. Sculpture, often of a high class, carving of every sort, tracery, and panelling, are largely employed; but with a hardness and a tendency to cover all surfaces with a profusion of weak imitations of tracery that disfigures much of the masonry. The tracery became towards the latter part of the time intricate and unmeaning, and the interpenetrating mouldings already described, though of course intended to be ornamental, are more perplexing and confusing than pleasing: the carving exaggerates the natural markings of the foliage represented, and being thin, and very boldly undercut, resembles leaves beaten out in metal, rather than foliage happily and easily imitated in stone, which is what good architectural carving should be.

The use of coloured building materials and of inlays and mosaics does not prevail to any great extent in Germany, though stained glass is often to be found and coloured wall decoration occasionally.

FIG. 49.—ST. SEBALD'S CHURCH AT NUREMBERG. THE BRIDE'S
DOORWAY. (1303-1377.)

Construction and Design.

The marked peculiarities of construction by which the German Gothic buildings are most distinguished, are the prevalent high-pitched roofs, the vaulting with aisle vaults carried to the same height as in the centre, and the employment in certain districts of brick to the exclusion of stone, all of which have been already referred to. In a great part of that large portion of Europe, which is included under the name of Germany, the materials and modes of construction adopted during the middle ages, bear a close resemblance to those in general use in France and England.

Some of the characteristics of German Gothic design have been already alluded to. The German architects display an exuberant fancy, a great love of the picturesque, and even the grotesque, and a strong predilection for creating artificial difficulties in order to enjoy the pleasure of surmounting them. Their work is full of unrest; they attach small value to the artistic quality of breadth, and destroy the value of the plain surfaces of their buildings as contrasts to the openings, by cutting them up by mouldings and enrichments of various sorts. The sculpture introduced is, as a rule, naturalistic rather than conventional. The capitals of piers and columns are often fine specimens of effective carving, while the delicate and ornamental details of the tabernacle work with which church furniture is enriched, are unsurpassed in elaboration, and often of rare beauty. The churches of Nuremberg are specially distinguished for the richness and number of their sculptured fittings. There is, moreover, in some of the best German buildings a rugged grandeur which approaches the sublime; and in the humbler ones a large amount of picturesque and thoroughly successful architecture.

In the smaller objects upon which the art of the architect was often employed the Germans were frequently happy. Public fountains, such for example as the one illustrated in Chapter II. (Fig. 10), are to be met within the streets of many towns, and rarely fail to please by their simple, graceful, and often quaint design. Crosses, monuments, and individual features in domestic buildings, such *e.g.* as bay windows, frequently show a very skilful and picturesque treatment and happy enrichment.

NORTHERN EUROPE.

2. Northern Europe

Gothic architecture closely resembling German work may be found in Switzerland, Norway and Sweden, and Denmark; but there are few very conspicuous buildings, and not enough variety to form a distinct style. In Norway and Sweden curious and picturesque buildings exist, erected solely of timber, and both there and in Switzerland many of the traditions of the Gothic period have been handed down to our own day with comparatively little change, in the pleasing and often highly enriched timber buildings which are to be met with in considerable numbers in those countries.

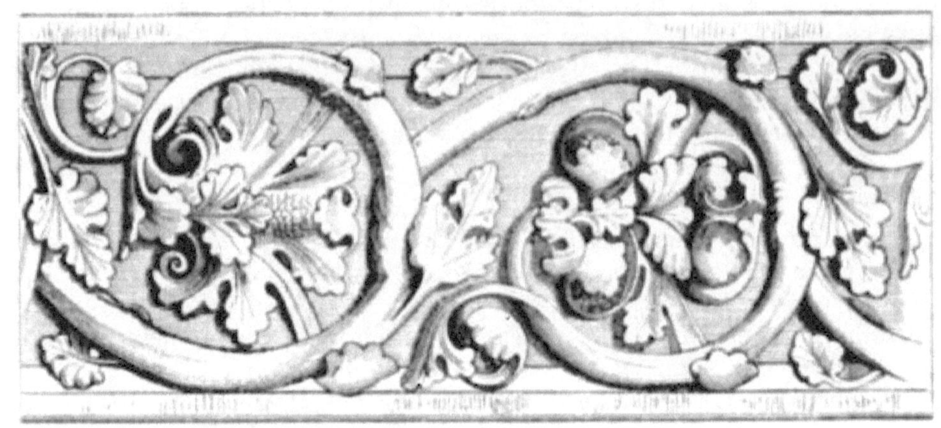

CHAPTER VIII.

GOTHIC ARCHITECTURE IN SOUTHERN EUROPE.

ITALY AND SICILY.—TOPOGRAPHICAL SKETCH.

1. Italy and Sicily. Topographical Sketch. Northern Italy. Central Italy. Southern Italy. Analysis of Buildings. Plans. Walls, Towers, and Columns. Openings and Arches. Roofs and Vaults. Mouldings and Ornaments. Construction and Design

GOTHIC architecture in Italy may be considered as a foreign importation. The Italians, it is true, displayed their natural taste and artistic instinct in their use of the style, and a large number of their works possess, as we shall see, strongly-marked characteristics and much charm; but it is impossible to avoid the feeling that the architects were working in a style not thoroughly congenial to their instincts nor to the traditions they had inherited from classical times; and not entirely in harmony with the requirements of the climate and the nature of their building materials.

Italian Gothic may be conveniently considered geographically, dividing the buildings into three groups, the first and most important containing the architecture of Northern Italy (Lombardy, Venetia, and the neighbourhood), the second that of Central Italy (Tuscany, &c.), the third that of the south and of Sicily—a classification which will suit the subject better than the chronological arrangement which has been our guide in examining the art of other countries; for the variations occasioned by development as time went on are less strongly marked in Italy than elsewhere.

Northern Italy.

Lombardy in the Romanesque period was thoroughly under German influence, and the buildings remaining to us from the eleventh and twelfth centuries bear a close resemblance to those erected north of the Alps at the same date. The twelfth century Lombard churches again are specimens of round-arched Gothic, just as truly as those on the banks of the Rhine. Many of them are also peculiar as being erected chiefly in brickwork; the great alluvial plain of Lombardy being deficient in building-stone. St. Michele at Pavia, a well-known church of this date, may be cited as a good example. This is a vaulted church, with an apsidal east end and transepts. The round arch is employed in this building, but the general proportions and treatment are essentially Gothic. A striking campanile (bell tower) belongs to the church, and is a good specimen of a feature very frequently met with in Lombardy; the tower here (and usually) is square, and rises by successive stages, but with only few and small openings or ornaments, to a considerable height. There are no buttresses, no diminution of bulk, no staircase turrets. At the summit is an open belfry-stage, with large semicircular-headed arches, crowned by a cornice and a low-pitched conical roof.[27]

In the same city a good example of an Italian Gothic church, erected after the pointed arch had been introduced, may be found in the church of Sta. Maria del Carmine. The west front of this church is but clumsy in general design. Its width is divided into five compartments by flat buttresses. The gables are crowned by a deep and heavy cornice of moulded brick and the openings are grouped with but little skill. Individually, however, the features of this front are very beautiful, and the great wheel-window, full of tracery, and the two-light windows flanking it, may be quoted as remarkable specimens of the ornamental elaboration which can be accomplished in brickwork.

The campanile of this church, like the one just described, is a plain square tower. It rises by successive stages, each taller than the last, each stage being marked by a rich brick cornice. The belfry-stage has on each face a three-light window, with a traceried head, and above the cornice the square tower is finished by a tall conical roof, circular on plan, an arrangement not unfrequently met with.

The Certosa, the great Carthusian Church and Monastery near Pavia,[28] best known by the elaborate marble front added in a different style about a century after the erection of the main building, is a good example of a highly-enriched church, with dependencies, built in brickwork, and possessing most of the distinctive peculiarities of a great Gothic church, except the general use of the pointed arch. It was begun in 1396, and is consistent in its exterior architecture, the front excepted, though it took a long time to build. Attached to it are two cloisters, of which the arches are semicircular, and the enrichments, of wonderful beauty, are modelled in terra-cotta.

This church resembles the great German round-arched Gothic churches on the Rhine in many of its features. Its plan includes a nave, with aisles and side chapels,

[27] An illustration of such a campanile will be found in that belonging to the Cathedral of Siena (Fig. 52).

[28] See Frontispiece.

transepts and a choir. The eastern arm and the transepts are each ornamented by an apse, somewhat smaller than would be met with in a German church; but as a compensation each of these three arms has two side apses, as well as the one at the end. The exterior possesses the German arcade of little arches immediately under the eaves of the roof; it is marked by the same multiplicity of small towers, each with its own steep roof; and it possesses the same striking central feature, internally a small dome, externally a kind of light pyramidal structure, ornamented by small arcades rising tier above tier, and ending in a central pointed roof.

The finest Gothic cathedral in North Italy, if dimensions, general effectiveness, and beauty of material be the test, is that of Milan. This building is disfigured by a west front in a totally inappropriate style, but apart from this it is virtually a German church of the first class, erected entirely in white marble, and covered with a profusion of decoration. Its dimensions show that, with the exception of Seville, this was the largest of all the Gothic cathedrals of Europe. It has double aisles, transepts, and a polygonal apse. At the crossing of the nave and transepts a low dome rises, covered by a conical roof, and surmounted by an elegant marble spire.

The structure is vaulted throughout, and each of the great piers which carry the nave arcade is surmounted by a mass of niches and tabernacle work, occupied by statues—a splendid substitute for ordinary capitals. The interior effect of Milan Cathedral is grand and full of beauty. The exterior, though much of its power is destroyed by the weakly-designed ornament with which all the surfaces of the walls are covered, is endowed with a wonderful charm. This building was commenced in the year 1385, and consecrated in the year 1418. The details of the window-tracery, pinnacles, &c. (but not the statues which are of Italian character), correspond very closely to those of German buildings erected at the same period (close of the fourteenth century).

Milan possesses, among other examples of pointed architecture, one secular building, the Great Hospital, well known for its Gothic façade. This hospital was founded in 1456, and most of it is of later date and of renaissance character; the street front of two storeys in height, with pointed arches, is very rich. The church of Chiaravalle, near Milan, which has been more than once illustrated and described, ought not to be passed unnoticed, on account of the beauty of its fully developed central dome. It was built in the early part of the thirteenth century (1221).

Almost all the great cities of North Italy possess striking Gothic buildings. Genoa, for instance, can boast of her cathedral, with a front in alternate courses of black and white marble, dating from about the year 1300, and full of beauty; the details bearing much resemblance to the best Western Gothic work. Passing eastward, Verona possesses a wealth of Gothic work in the well-known tombs of the Scaligers, the churches of Sta. Anastasia, San Zenone, and several minor churches and campaniles; and at Como, Bergamo, Vicenza, Padua, Treviso, Cremona, Bologna, and many other cities and towns, good churches of pointed architecture are to be found.

Our illustration (Fig. 50) of the ancient Palace of the Jurisconsults at Cremona, is a good specimen of the secular architecture of North Italy. Originally the lower storey was a loggia, or open arcaded storey, but the arches have been built up. Telling, simple, and graceful, this building owes its effect chiefly to its well-designed openings and a characteristic brick cornice. It is entirely without buttresses, has no spreading base, no gables, and no visible roof: some of these features would have been present had it been designed and erected north of the Alps.

FIG. 50.—THE PALACE OF THE JURISCONSULTS AT CREMONA.

Venice is the city in the whole of North Italy where Gothic architecture has had freest scope and has achieved the greatest success, not, however, in ecclesiastical, but in secular buildings. The great Cathedral of St. Mark, perhaps the most wonderful church in Europe, certainly the foremost in Italy, is a Byzantine building, and though it has received some additions in Gothic times, does not fairly come within the scope of this volume; and the Gothic churches of Venice are not very numerous nor, with the exception of the fine brick church of the Frari, extremely remarkable. On the banks of the Grand Canal and its tributaries, however, stand not a few Gothic palaces of noble design (see Fig. 9, p. 18), while the Ducal Palace itself alone is sufficient to confer a reputation upon the city which it adorns.

The Ducal Palace at Venice is a large rectangular block of buildings erected round a vast quadrangle. Of its exterior two sides only are visible from a distance, one being the sea front looking over the lagoon, and the other the land front directed towards the piazzetta. Rather less than one half the height of each front is occupied by two storeys of arcades; the lower storey bold, simple, and vigorous; the upper storey lighter, and ending in a mass of bold tracery. Above this open work, and resting upon it, rises the external wall of the palace, faced with marble in alternate slabs of rose-colour and white, pierced by a few large pointed windows and crowned by an open parapet. Few buildings are so familiar, even to untravelled persons, as this fine work, which owes its great charm to the extent, beauty, and mingled solidity and grace of its arcades, and to the fine sculpture by which the capitals from which they spring are enriched.

The Gothic palaces are almost invariably remarkable for the skill with which the openings in their fronts are arranged and designed. It was not necessary to render any other part of the exterior specially architectural, as the palaces stand side by side like houses in a modern street, as can be seen from our illustration (Fig. 9). In almost all cases a large proportion of the openings are grouped together in the centre of the front, and the sides are left comparatively plain and strong-looking, the composition presenting a centre and two wings. By this simple expedient each portion of the composition is made to add emphasis to the other, and a powerful but not inharmonious contrast between the open centre and the solid sides is called into existence. The earliest Gothic buildings in point of date are often the most delicate and graceful, and this rule holds good in the Gothic palaces of Venice; yet one of the later palaces, the Ca' d'Oro, must be at least named on account of the splendid richness of its marble front—of which, however, only the centre and one wing is built—and the beauty of the ornament lavishly employed upon it.

The balconies, angle windows, and other minor features with which the Venetian Gothic palaces abound, are among the most graceful features of the architecture of Italy.

Central Italy.

Those towns of Central Italy (by which is meant Tuscany and the former States of the Church), in which the best Gothic buildings are to be found, are Pisa, Lucca, Florence, Siena, Orvieto, and Perugia. As a general rule the Gothic work in this district is more developed and more lavishly enriched than that in Lombardy.

In Pisa, the Cathedral and the Campanile (the famous leaning tower) belong to the late Romanesque style, but the Baptistry, an elegant circular building, has a good deal of Gothic ornament in its upper storeys, and may be fairly classed as a transitional building. The most charming and thoroughly characteristic work of Gothic architecture in Pisa is, however, a small gem of a chapel, the church of Sta. Maria della Spina. It displays exquisite ornament, and, notwithstanding much false construction, the beauty of its details, of its sculpture, and of the marble of which it is built, invest it with a great charm.

Pisan Gothic is remarkable as being associated with the name of a family of highly gifted sculptors and architects, the Pisani, of whom Nicola Pisano was the earliest and greatest artist; he was followed by his descendants Giovanni, Nino, and Andrea. With the Pisani and Giotto the series of the known names of architects of great buildings may be said to begin.

Florence, the most important of the cities we have named, is distinguished by a cathedral built in the early part of the fourteenth century, and one of the grandest in Italy. It has very few columns, and its walls and vaults are of great height. The walls are adorned externally with inlays in coloured marble, and the windows have stained glass—a rarity in Italy; but its lofty dome, added after the completion of the rest of the building, is its chief feature. This was always intended, but the pointed octagonal dome actually erected by Brunelleschi, between the years 1420 and 1444, though it harmonises fairly well with the general lines of the building, and forms, as can be seen from our illustration (Fig. 51), a striking object in all distant views of the city, is probably very different from what was originally intended. Near the cathedral stand the Baptistry, famous for the possession of the finest gates in the world, and the Campanile of Giotto. This tower is built, or at least faced, entirely with marble; and when it is stated that its height is not far short of that of the Victoria Tower of our Houses of Parliament, though of slenderer proportions, it will be seen that it is magnificently liberal in its general scheme. The tower is covered with panels of variously coloured marbles from base to summit, and enriched by fine sculpture. The angles are strengthened by slightly projecting piers. The windows are comparatively small till the highest or belfry stage is reached, and here each face of the tower is pierced by a magnificent three-light window. A deep and elaborate cornice now crowns the whole, but it was originally designed to add a high-pitched roof or a spire as a terminal.

FIG. 51.—THE CATHEDRAL AT FLORENCE. WITH GIOTTO'S CAMPANILE.

(Begun, 1298; Dome, 1420-1444; Campanile begun, 1324.)

Our illustration (Fig. 52) shows the west front and campanile of the Cathedral at Siena, an exceedingly good specimen of the beauties and peculiarities of the style. This building was commenced in 1243. The plan is simple but singular, for the central feature is a six-sided dome, at the crossing of the nave and transepts; and some ingenuity has been spent in fitting this figure to the arches of the main avenues of the building. The interior is rich and effective; the exterior, as can be seen by the illustration, is covered with ornament, and the front is the richest and probably the best designed of all the cathedral fronts of Central Italy. The strongly-marked horizontal lines of cornices, arcades, &c., the moulded gables, the great wheel-window set in a square panel, and the use of marble of various colours, are all points to note. So is the employment of the semicircular arch for the doorways of this thoroughly Gothic building. The campanile is a good example of that feature, except that instead of the rich window which usually occupies the belfry stage, or highest storey, two storeys of small lights have been formed. The introduction of angle turrets is not very usual, and it here supplies a deficiency which makes itself felt in other campaniles, where the junction of tower and spire is not always happy.

FIG. 52.—CATHEDRAL AT SIENA. WEST FRONT AND CAMPANI-
LE.

(Façade begun 1284.)

Gothic churches of importance can be found in many of the cities and towns of Central Italy. None are more remarkable than the singular double church of St. Francis at Assisi, with its wealth of mural paintings and stained glass, and the cathedral at Orvieto (Fig. 53) with its splendid front.

In Rome, so rich in specimens of the architecture of many styles and times, Gothic could find no footing; the one solitary church which can be claimed as Gothic may be taken as an exception. And south of the Capital there lies a considerable tract of country, containing few if any examples of the style we are considering.

Southern Italy.

Southern Italy is conveniently grouped with Sicily, but the mainland is deficient in examples of Gothic buildings. The old towns of Apulia indeed, such as Bari, Bitonto and Brindisi, possess an architecture which the few who have had an opportunity of examining, declare to be surpassingly rich in its decoration, but it is for the most part Romanesque.

The Gothic work remaining in and about Naples is most of it extremely florid, and often rich, but seldom possesses the grace and charm of that which exists further north.

Sicily shows the picturesquely mixed results of a complication of agencies which have not affected the mainland, and is accordingly an interesting field for architectural study. The island was first under Byzantine influence; was next occupied and held by the Saracens; and was later seized and for some time retained by the Normans.

FIG. 53.—THE CATHEDRAL AT ORVIETO. (BEGUN 1290; FAÇADE, 1310.)

The most striking early Gothic building in Sicily is the richly adorned cathedral of Monreale, commenced in the twelfth century. Here very simple pointed arches are made use of, as the entire surface of the interior is covered with mosaic pictures of Norman origin. The small Capella Palatina in Palermo itself is of the same simple and early architectural character, and adorned with equally magnificent mosaics. In these buildings the splendour of the colouring is only equalled by the vigorous and often pathetic power with which the stories of sacred history are embodied in these mosaics. The cathedral of Cefalu is a building bearing a general resemblance to that at Monreale, but not enriched in the same manner.

Of the fourteenth century are the richly ornamented cathedral of Palermo and that of Messina. The latter has been so much altered as to have lost a good deal of its interest; but at Palermo there is much that is striking and almost unique. This building has little in common with the works of northern or central Italy, and not much more alliance with the Gothic of North Europe. It is richly panelled and decorated, but its most striking feature is its bold arcaded portal.

ANALYSIS OF BUILDINGS.

Plan.

The plans of Italian churches are simple, compared with those of the northern and western architects. As a rule they are also moderate in size, and they bear a close resemblance to those of the early basilica churches from which they are directly descended. Though the apse is all but universal, the French *chevet*, with its crown of clustering chapels, was not adopted in Italy. There is very much in common between the churches of Lombardy and those of Germany, but the German western apse and the apsidal ends to the transept do not occur. The spaces between the piers of the main arcade are greater than in French or English examples, so that there are fewer piers, and the vaults are of wider span. In the churches founded by the great preaching orders, the division into nave and aisle does not take place, and the church consists of nothing but a large hall for the congregation, with a chancel for the choir.

In monastic, secular, and domestic building a general squareness and simplicity of plan prevails, and where an internal arcaded quadrangle can be made use of (*e.g.* in the cloister of a monastery), it is almost always relied upon to add effect. The famous external arcade at the Ducal Palace, Venice, was nowhere repeated, though simpler external arcades occur frequently; but it is so splendid as to form, itself alone a feature in Italian planning.

The arrangements of the mansions and palaces found in the great cities were a good deal influenced by the circumstance that it was customary, in order to secure as much cool air as possible, to devote one of the upper floors to the purpose of a suite of reception rooms; to this was given the name of *piano nobile*.

Walls, Towers, Columns.

Walls are usually thick and stand unbuttressed, and rarely have such slopes and diminutions of apparent thickness towards their upper part as are not uncommon in England. Base mouldings are not universal. The cornice, on the other hand, is far more cared for, and is made much more conspicuous than with us. In the brick buildings especially it attains great development. Above the cornice a kind of ornamental parapet, bearing some resemblance to battlements, is common. The strikingly peculiar use of materials of different colours in alternate courses, or in panels, to decorate the wall surfaces, has already been referred to. It is very characteristic of the style.

The campanile or bell-tower of an Italian church is a feature very different from western towers. It is never placed over the crossing of nave and aisles and rarely forms an essential part of the church, often being quite detached and not seldom placed at an angle with the walls of the main building. Such towers are not unfrequently appended to palaces, and are sometimes (*e.g.* at Venice) erected alone. Some of the Italian cities were also remarkable for strong towers erected in the city itself as fortresses by the heads of influential families. Many of these are still standing in Bologna. The smaller towers in which northern architects took so much delight are almost unknown in Italy, though on a few of the great churches of the north (*e.g.* the Certosa at Pavia, and St. Antonio at Padua) they are to be found.

The use of constructive columns is general; piers are by no means unknown, but fine shafts of marble meet the eye frequently in Italian churches. The constant use of the column for decorative purposes is a marked characteristic. Not only is it employed where French and English architects used it, as in the jambs of doorways, but it constantly replaces the mullion in traceried windows. It is employed as an ornament at the angles of buildings to take off the harshness of a sharp corner, and it is introduced in many unexpected and often picturesque situations. Twisted, knotted, and otherwise carved and ornamental shafts are not unfrequently made use of in columns that serve purely decorative purposes.

Openings and Arches.

The constructive arches in Italian Gothic buildings are, as a rule, pointed, but it is remarkable that at every period round and pointed arches are indiscriminately employed for doors and windows, both being constantly met with in the same building.

The naves of Italian churches rarely show the division into three, common in the north. The triforium is almost invariably absent, and the clerestory is often reduced to a series of small round windows, sufficient to admit the moderate light which, in a very bright climate, is grateful in the interior of such a building as a church; but they are far less effective features than our own well-marked clerestory windows.

FIG. 54.—OGIVAL WINDOW-HEAD.

The doorways are often very beautiful, and are frequently sheltered by projecting porches of extreme elegance and lightness. The window openings are, as a rule, cusped. An ogee-shaped arch (Fig. 54) is constantly in use in window-heads, especially at Venice, and much graceful design is lavished on the arched openings of domestic and secular buildings. A great deal of the tracery employed is plate tracery.[29] The tracery in terra-cotta has already been referred to. In the large windows of the principal apartments and other similar positions of the palaces in Venice and Vicenza, a sort of tracery not met with in other countries is freely employed. The openings are square-headed, and are divided into separate lights by small columns; the heads of these lights are ogee-shaped, and the spaces between them and the horizontal lintel are filled in with circles, richly quatrefoiled or otherwise cusped (Fig. 55). The upper arcade of the Ducal Palace at Venice offers the best known and finest example of this class of tracery.

FIG. 55.—TRACERY, FROM VENICE.

Roofs and Vaults.

The vaulting of Italian churches is always simple, and the bays, as has been pointed out, are usually wider than those of the northern Gothic churches. Frequently there are no ribs of any sort to the groins of the vaults. A characteristic feature of Italian Gothic is the central dome. It is rarely very large or overpowering, and in the one instance of a magnificent dome—the Cathedral at Florence, the feature, though intended from the first, was added after the Gothic period had closed. Still many churches have a modest dome, and it frequently forms a striking feature in the interior, while in some northern instances (*e.g.* at the Certosa at Pavia, or at Chiaravalle) it is treated like a many storeyed pyramid and becomes

---

[29] For an explanation of this term, see *ante*, Chapter V., page 48.

an external feature of importance. At Sant' Antonio at Padua there are five domes.

The churches of the preaching orders are some of them covered by timber ceilings, not perfectly flat but having an outline made up of hollow curves of rather flat sweep. The great halls at Padua and Vicenza displayed a vast wooden curved ceiling resembling the hull of a ship turned upside down.

The ordinary church roof is of flat pitch and frequently concealed behind a parapet. Dormer windows, crestings, and other similar features, by the use of which northern architects enriched their roofs, are hardly ever employed by Italian architects.

Mouldings and Ornaments.

Ornament is almost instinctively understood by the Italians, and their mastery of it is well shown in their architecture. The carving of spandrels, capitals, and other ornaments, and the sculpture of the heads and statues introduced is full of power and beauty. The famous capitals of the lower arcade of the Ducal Palace may be quoted as illustrations.

The employment of coloured materials is carried so far as sometimes to startle an eye trained to the sombreness of English architecture, but a great deal of the beauty of this style is derived from colour, and much of the comparative simplicity and scarcity of mouldings is due to the desire to leave large unbroken surfaces for marble linings, mosaics or fresco painting. Mouldings, where they are introduced, differ from northern mouldings in being flatter and far less bold, their enrichments are chiefly confined to dentils, notches, and small and simple ornaments. Stained glass is not so often seen as in France, but is to be met with, as, for example, in the fine church of San Petronio at Bologna, and in Sta. Maria Novella, and in the Cathedral at Florence. At Florence the stained glass has a character of its own both in colour and style of treatment. It is not too much to say that every kind of decoration which can be employed to add beauty to a building may be found at its best in Italy. In the churches much of the finest furniture, such as stall-work, screens, altar frontals, will be found in profusion; and the church porches and the mural monuments should be especially studied on account of the singular elegance with which they are usually designed.

Construction and Design.

The material employed for the external and internal face of the walls in a very large proportion of the buildings mentioned in this chapter is marble. This is sometimes used in blocks as stone is with us, but more frequently in the form of thin slabs as a facing upon masonry or brickwork. In Lombardy, where brick is the natural building material, most of the walls are not only built but faced with brick; and the ornamental features, including tracery, are often executed in ornamental brickwork, or in what is known as terra-cotta (*i.e.* bricks or blocks of brick clay of fine quality, moulded or otherwise ornamented and burnt like bricks). Stone was less commonly employed as a building material in Italy during the Gothic period, than in other countries of Europe. The surfaces of the vaults, and the surfaces of the internal walls were often covered with mosaics, or with paintings in fresco. Vaulting is frequently met with, but it is generally simple in character, the flat external roof over it is commonly covered with tiles or metal, while the apparent gable frequently rises more sharply than the actual roof. The Italians seem never to have cordially welcomed the Gothic principle of resisting the thrust of vaults or arches by a counter-thrust, or by the weight of a buttress. The buttress is almost unknown in Italian Gothic, and as a rule an iron tie is introduced at the feet of such arches as would in France or Germany have been buttressed. This expedient is, of course, economical, but to northern eyes it appears strange and out of place. The Italians, however, take no pains to conceal it, and many of their lighter works, such as canopies over tombs, porches, &c., would fall to pieces at once were the iron ties removed.

Open timber roofs in the English fashion are unknown; but the wooden ceilings already alluded to are found in San Zeno at Verona, and the Eremitani at Padua. A kind of open roof of large span, carried by curved ribs and tied by iron ties, covers the great hall of the Basilica at Vicenza, and the very similar hall at Padua. The ribs of these roofs are built up of many thicknesses of material bolted together.

The design of Italian Gothic buildings presents many peculiarities, some of which are due to the materials made use of. For example, where brick and terra-cotta are alone employed, wide moulded cornices of no great projection, and broad masses of enriched moulding encircling arches are easily executed, and they are accordingly constantly to be found; but bold mouldings, with deep hollows, similar to those of Early English arches, could not be constructed of these materials, and are not attempted. These peculiarities will be found in the Town Hall at Cremona, of which an illustration (Fig. 50) has already been given.

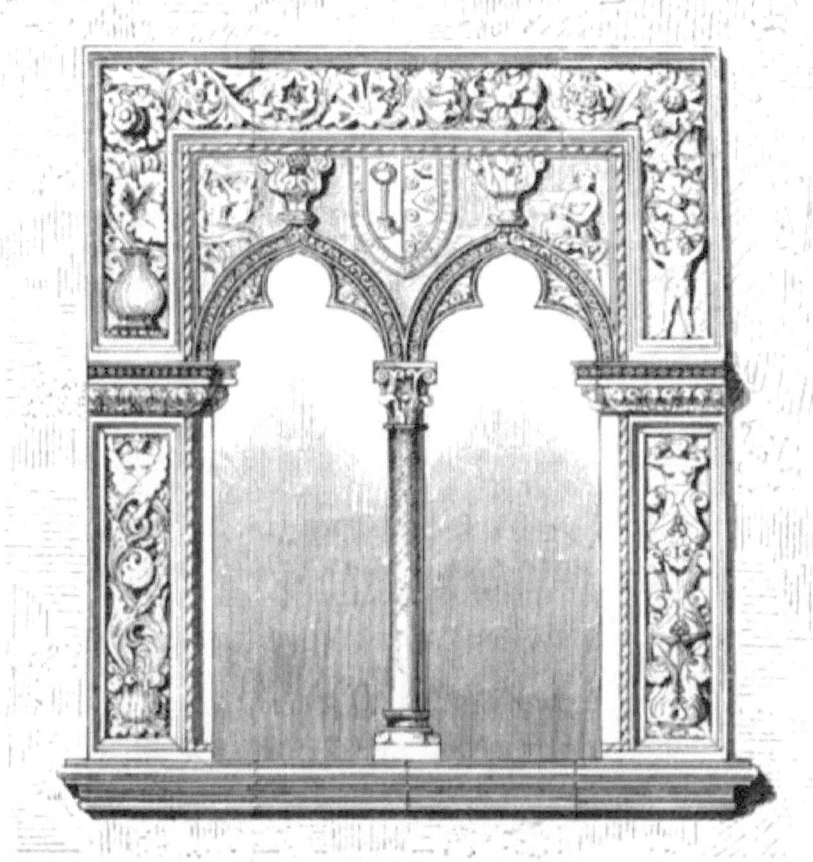

FIG. 56.—WINDOW FROM TIVOLI.

Where marble is used, the peculiar fineness of its surface, upon which the bright Italian sun makes the smallest moulding effective, combined with the fact that the material, being costly, is often used in thin slabs, has given occasion to extreme flatness of treatment, and to the use of modes of enrichment which do not require much depth of material. Our illustration of a window from the Piazza S. Croce at Tivoli, shows these peculiarities extremely well (Fig. 56), and also illustrates the strong predilection which the Italian architects retained throughout the Gothic period for squareness and for horizontal lines. The whole ornamental treatment is here square; the window rests on a strongly-moulded horizontal sill, and is surrounded by flatly-carved enrichment, making a square panel of the entire feature. Even in the richly-decorated window (Fig. 57), which is in its pointed outline more truly Gothic than the Tivoli example, much of the same quality can be traced. The arch and jamb are richly moulded, but the whole mass of mouldings is flat, and the flat cuspings of the tracery, elaborately carved though it be, more resemble the cusps of early Western Gothic, executed at a time when tracery was beginning its career, than work belonging to the period of full maturity to which this feature, as a whole, undoubtedly belongs.

Where marbles were plentiful enough to be built into the fabric, the national love of colour gave rise to the use of black and white—or sometimes red and white—alternate courses, already mentioned. The effect of this striped masonry may be partly judged of from the illustration of the cathedral at Siena (Fig. 52), where it is employed to a considerable extent. A finer method of surface decoration, less simple, however, and perhaps less frequently practised, was open to the Italian architect, in the use of panels of various coloured marbles. A beautiful example of the employment of this expedient exists in Giotto's campanile at Florence (Fig. 51).

FIG. 57.—ITALIAN GOTHIC WINDOW, WITH TRACERY IN THE HEAD.

(13th Century.)

The flatness of the roofs, which the Italians never abandoned, was always found difficult to reconcile with the Gothic tendency to height and steepness. In many cases, the sharp pitched gables which the buildings display, are only masks, and do not truly denote the pitch of the roofs behind them. In other instances the walls finish with a horizontal parapet, plain or ornamental, quite concealing the roof. In the roofs of their campaniles, however, the Gothic architects of Italy were usually happy; they almost always adopted a steep conical terminal, with or without pinnacles, which is very telling against the sky; even if its junction with the tower is at times clumsy.

The brightness of southern suns prevented the adoption of the great windows, adapted to masses of stained glass, which were the ambition of northern architects in the fourteenth century; and the tenacity with which a love for squareness of effect and for strongly-marked horizontal lines of various sorts retained its hold, tended to keep Italian Gothic buildings essentially different from those of northern nations; but the love of colour, the command of precious materials, and of fine sculpture, the passion for beauty and for a decorative richness, and the artistic taste of the Italians, display themselves in these buildings in a hundred ways: all this lends to them a charm such as few works of the middle ages existing elsewhere can surpass.

SPAIN.—CHRONOLOGICAL SKETCH.

2. Spain. Chronological Sketch

An early, middle, and late period can be distinguished in dealing with Spanish Gothic. The first period reaches to the first quarter of the thirteenth century, the second occupies the remainder of the thirteenth and the fourteenth centuries, the third completes the fifteenth and runs on into part of the sixteenth.

The early style is one of much purity and dignity, and is developed directly from the Romanesque of the country. The cathedral of St. Iago di Compostella, a fine cruciform church of round-arched Gothic, with a magnificent western portal,[30] recalling the great lateral porches at Chartres, is an early and fine example. Like other churches of the type in Spain, it is far plainer inside than out, but it is vaulted throughout.

The cathedral of Zamora, and those of Tarragona and Salamanca must also be referred to. In each of these, the most thoroughly Spanish feature is a dome, occupying the crossing of the nave and transepts, and apparently better developed than those in early German churches or in Italian ones. It is called in Spanish the *cimborio*. This feature was constructed so as to consist of an inner dome, decorated by ribs thrown over the central space, and carried by pendentives; having above it a separate outer dome somewhat higher and often richly decorated. This feature unfortunately disappeared when the French designs of the thirteenth century began to be the rage. A peculiarity of plan, however, which was retained throughout the whole Gothic period in Spain, is to be found in the early churches; it consists of an inclosure for the choir quite in the body of the church, and often west of the transepts,—in such a position, in fact, as the choir at Westminster Abbey occupies. A third peculiarity is the addition of an outer aisle, not unlike the arcade of a cloister, to the side walls of the churches, possibly with a view of protecting them from heat.

With the thirteenth century a strong passion for churches, closely resembling those being erected in France at the same time, set in, as has just been remarked.

[30] A cast of this portal is at the South Kensington Museum.

Accordingly the cathedrals of Toledo, Burgos, and Leon, approach very closely to French types. Toledo is very large, five aisled, and with a vast chevet. Its exterior is unfinished, but the dignity of its fine interior may be well understood from the illustration (Fig. 58) here given. Burgos is not so ambitious in size as Toledo, but has a florid exterior of late architecture with two lofty, open-traceried spires, like Strasburg and other German examples. Leon is remarkable for its lofty clerestory. Spanish Gothic may be said to have culminated in the vast cathedral at Seville (begun 1401), claiming to be of greater extent than any Gothic cathedral in the world, larger, therefore, than Milan or Cologne. It stands on the site of a mosque, and has never been completed externally. The interior is very imposing and rich, but when it is stated that it was not completed till 1520, it may be readily understood that many of the details are very late, and far from the purity of earlier examples.

FIG. 58.—THE CATHEDRAL AT TOLEDO. INTERIOR. (BEGUN 1227.)

In the fourteenth century an innovation, of which French architects immediately north of the Pyrenees were also availing themselves, found favour in Barcelona. The great buttresses by which the thrust of the vaults was met were brought inside the boundary walls of the church, and were made to serve as division walls between a series of side chapels. Both here and at Manresa and Gerona, cathedrals were built, resembling in construction that at Alby, in Southern France; in these this arrangement was carried a step further, and the side aisles were suppressed, leaving the whole nave to consist of a very bold vaulted hall, fringed by a series of side chapels, which were separated from each other by the buttresses which supported the main vault. These large vaults, however, when bare of decoration, as most of the Spanish vaults are, appear bald and poor in effect, though they are grand objects structurally.

The Gothic work of the latest period in Spain became extraordinarily florid in its details, especially in the variety introduced into the ribs of the vaulting and the enrichments generally. The great cathedrals of Segovia and Salamanca were neither of them begun till the sixteenth century had already well set in. They are the two principal examples of this florid Gothic.

FIG. 59.—THE GIRALDA AT SEVILLE. (BEGUN IN 1196. FINISHED IN 1538).

It will not be forgotten that the country we are now considering was fully occupied by the Moors, and that they left in Southern Spain buildings of great merit. A certain number of Christian churches exist built in a style which has been called Moresco, as being a kind of fusion of Moorish and Gothic. The towers of these churches bear a close resemblance to the Saracenic towers of which the beautiful bell-tower, called the Giralda, at Seville (Fig. 59) is the type; with this and similar examples in the country it is not surprising that at Toledo, Saragoza, and other places, towers of the same character should be erected as parts of churches in which the architecture throughout is as much Saracenic as Christian.

To many of these great churches, cloisters, and monastic buildings, which are often both extensive and of a high order of architectural excellence, are attached. The secular buildings, of Spain in the Gothic period are, on the other hand, neither numerous nor remarkable.

PORTUGAL.

3. Portugal

The architecture of Portugal has been very little investigated. The great church at Batalha[31] is probably the most important in the country. This building, though interesting in plan, is more remarkable for a lavish amount of florid ornament, of which our illustration (Fig. 60) may furnish some idea, than for really fine architecture. The conventual church at Belem, near Lisbon, a work of the beginning of the sixteenth century, and equally florid, is another of the small number of specimens of Portuguese Gothic of which descriptions or illustrations have been published.

---

[31] See *Sculptures of the Monastery at Batalha*, published by the Arundel Society.

CHAPTER IX.

GOTHIC ARCHITECTURE.

Principles of Construction and Design. Materials and Construction

Materials and Construction.

THE Gothic architects adhered, at any rate till the fifteenth century, to the use of very small stones in their masonry. In many buildings of large size it is hard to find any stone heavier than two men can lift. Bad roads and the absence of good mechanical means of hoisting and moving big blocks led to this.

The mortar, though good, is not equal to the Roman. As a rule in each period mortar joints are thick. They are finest in the fifteenth century.

The masonry of all important features of the building is always good; it is often a perfect marvel of dexterity and skill as well as of beauty.

The arts of workers in other materials, such as carpenters, joiners, smiths, and plumbers were carried to great perfection during the Gothic period.

The appropriate ornamental treatment which each material is best fitted to receive was invariably given to it, and forms appropriate to one material were very rarely copied in others. For example, whenever wrought iron, a material which can be beaten and welded, or rivetted, was employed, those ornamental forms were selected into which hot iron can with ease be beaten, and such groups of those forms were designed as can be obtained by welding or by rivetting them together.

Wood, on the other hand, cannot be bent with ease, but can be readily cut, drilled with holes, notched and carved; accordingly, where wood had to be treated ornamentally, we only find such forms as the drill, the chisel, the saw, or the gouge readily and naturally leave behind them.

Again, the mode into which wood can be best framed together was carefully considered from a constructional point of view, and mediæval joiners' work is always first so designed as to reduce the damage from shrinkage to the smallest amount possible; and the pieces of which it is composed are then appropriately ornamented, moulded, or carved.

Stone is now always, at least in this country, worked by being first squared and then worked-down or "sunk" from the squared faces to the mouldings required, and this procedure seems to have been common, though not quite universal, in the Middle Ages. Consequently we usually find the whole of the external mouldings with which the doorways and arcades of important buildings were enriched, designed so as to be easily formed out of stones having squared faces, or, to use the technical phrase, to be "sunk" from the squared blocks.

The character of sculpture in wood differs from that in stone, the material being harder, more capable of standing alone; so in stone we find more breadth, in wood finer lines and more elaboration.

In a word, no material was employed in simulating another (or with the rarest exceptions), and when any ornament was to be executed in one place in one material and in another place in a different one, such alterations were always made in the treatment as corresponded to the different qualities of the two materials.

The arch was introduced whenever possible, and the structure of a great Gothic building presents the strongest possible contrast to that of a Greek building.

In the Greek temple there was no pressure that was not vertical and met by a vertical support, wall, or column, and no support that was not vastly in excess of the dimensions actually required to do the work.

A great Gothic building attains stability through the balanced counterpoise of a vast series of pressures, oblique, perpendicular, or horizontal, so arranged as to counteract each other. The vault was kept from spreading by the flying buttress, the thrust of the arcade was resisted by massive walls, and so on throughout.

The equilibrium thus obtained was sometimes so ticklish that a storm of wind, a trifling settlement, or a slight concussion sufficed to occasion a disaster; and many of the daring feats of the masons of the Middle Ages are lost to us, because they dared a little too much and the entire structure collapsed. This happened more often in the middle period of the style than in the earliest, but during the whole Gothic period there is a constant uniform tendency in one direction: thinner walls, wider arches, loftier vaults, slenderer buttresses, slighter piers, confront us at every step, and we need only compare some Norman structure (such as Durham), with a perpendicular (such as Henry VII.'s Chapel), to see how vast a change took place in this respect.

The Principles of Gothic Design.

All the germs of Gothic architecture exist in the Romanesque of the eleventh and twelfth centuries, and became developed as the passion for more slender proportions, greater lightness, and loftiness of effect, and more delicate enrichment became marked. It is quite true that the pointed arch is universally recognised as, so to speak, the badge of Gothic, even to the extent of having suggested the title of Christian pointed architecture, by which it is often called. But the pointed arch must be regarded rather as a token that the series of changes, which, starting from the heavy if majestic Romanesque of such a cathedral as Peterborough, culminated in the gracefulness of Salisbury or Lincoln, was far advanced towards completion, than as really essential to their perfection. Many of the examples of the transition period exhibit the round arch blended with the pointed (*e.g.* the nave of St. David's Cathedral or the Choir of Canterbury), and when we come to consider German architecture we shall find that the adoption of the pointed arch was postponed till long after the development of all, or almost all, the other features of the Gothic style; so as to place beyond question the existence, in that country at least, of "round arched Gothic." Some of the best authorities have indeed proposed to employ this title as a designation for much, if not all, the round arched architecture of the west of Europe, but Scott, Sharpe, and other authorities class mediæval art down to the middle of the twelfth century under the general head of Romanesque, a course which has been adopted in this volume.

The proportions of Gothic buildings were well studied, their forms were always lofty, their gables sharp, and their general composition more or less pyramidal. Remarkable numerical relations between the dimensions of the different parts of a great Gothic cathedral can be discovered upon careful examination in most, if not all instances, and there can be little doubt that a system of geometrical proportions ran through the earlier design, and that much of the harmony and beauty which the buildings present is traceable to this fact. Independent of this the skill with which subordinate features and important ones are fitted to their respective positions, both by their dimensions and by their relative elaboration or plainness, forms a complete system of proportion, making use of the word in its broadest sense; and the results are extremely happy.

Apparent size was imparted to almost every Gothic building by the smallness, great number, and variety of its features, and by the small size of the stones employed. The effect of strength is generally, though not perhaps so uniformly, also obtained, and dignity, beauty, and harmony are rarely wanting.

Symmetry, though not altogether overlooked, has but a slender hold upon Gothic architects. It is far more observed in the interior than in the exterior of the buildings; but it must be remembered that symmetry formed the basis of many designs which, owing to the execution having been carried on through a long series of years and by different hands, came to be varied from the original intentions. Thus, for example, Chartres is a cathedral with two western towers. One of these was carried up and its spire completed in the twelfth century. The companion spire was not added till the end of the fifteenth, when men's ideas as to the proportions, shape, ornaments, and details of a spire had altered entirely;—the later architect did not value symmetry enough to think himself bound to adhere either to the design or to the height of the earlier spire, so we have in this great façade two similar flanking towers but spires entirely unlike. What happened at Chartres happened elsewhere. The original design of buildings was in the main symmetrical, but it was never considered that symmetry was a matter so important as to require that much sacrifice should be made to preserve it.

On the other hand the subordination of a multitude of small features to one dominant one enters largely into the design of every good Gothic building; with the result that if the great governing feature or mass has been carried out in its entirety, almost any feature, no matter how irregular or unsymmetrical, may be safely introduced, and will only add picturesqueness and piquancy to the design. This is more or less a leading principle of Gothic design. A building with no irregularities, none of those charming additions which add individual character to Gothic churches, and none of the isolated features which the principle of subordination permits the architect to employ, has missed one of the chief qualities of the style. It is here that unskilled architects mostly fail when they attempt Gothic designs; they either hold on to symmetry as though they were designing a Greek temple, and they are unaware that the spirit of the style in which they are trying to work not only permits, but requires some irregular features; or if they do not fall into this error they are overtaken by the opposite one, and omit to make their irregular features subordinate to the general effect of the whole, an error less serious in its effects than the other, but still destructive of anything like the highest qualities in a building.

Repetition, like symmetry, is recognised by Gothic architecture, but not adhered to in a rigid way. No buildings gain more from the repetition of parts than Gothic churches and cathedrals; the series of pillars or piers and arches inside, the series of buttresses and windows outside, add scale to the general effect. But so long as it was in the main a series of features which broadly resembled one another, the Gothic architect was satisfied, and did not feel bound to exact repetition.

We are often, for example, surprised to find in the columns of a church an octagonal one alternating with a circular one, and almost invariably, if a series of capitals be examined, each will be discovered to differ from the others to some extent. In one bay of a church there may be a two-light window, and in the next a three-light window, and so on.

This we find in buildings erected at one time and under one architect. Where, however, a building begun at one period was continued at another (and this, it must be remembered, was the rule, not the exception, with all large Gothic buildings), the architect, while usually repeating the same features, with the same general forms, invariably followed his own predilections as to detail. There is a very good example of this in Westminster Abbey, in the western bays of the nave, which were built years later than the eastern bays. They are, to a superficial observer, identical, being of the same height and width and shape of arch, but nearly every detail differs.

Disclosure, rather than concealment, was a principle of Gothic design. This was demonstrated long ago by Pugin, and many of his followers pushed the doctrine to such extremes, that they held — and some of them still hold — that no building is really Gothic in which any part, either of its construction or arrangement, is not obviously visible inside and out.

This is, however, carrying the principle too far. It is sufficient to say that the interior disposition of every Gothic building was as much as possible disclosed by the exterior. Thus, in a secular building, where there is a large room, there usually was a large window; when a lofty apartment occurs, its roof was generally proportionately high; where a staircase rises, we usually can detect it by a sloping row of little windows following the line of the stair, or by a turret roof.

The mode in which the thrust of vaults is counterpoised is, as has been shown, frankly displayed by the Gothic architects, and as a rule, every portion of the structure is freely exhibited. It grows out of this, that when an ornamental feature is desired, it is not constructed purely for ornament, as the Romans added the columns and cornices of the orders to the outside of their massive walls purely as an architectural screen; but some requisite, of the building is taken and ornamented, and in some cases elaborated. Thus the belfry grew into the enormous bell tower; the tower roof grew into the spire; the extra weight required on flying buttresses grew into the ornamental pinnacle; and the window head grew into tracery.

There were, however, some exceptions. The walls were still constantly faced with finer masonry than in the heart, and though some are unwilling to admit the fact, were often plastered outside as well as in; and what is more remarkable, no other sign of the vault appeared outside the building than the buttresses required to sustain it.

The external gable conforms to the shape of the roof which covered the vault, but the vault, perhaps the most remarkable and characteristic feature of the whole building, does not betray its presence by any external line or mark corresponding to its position and shape in the interior of the building. Notwithstanding these and some other exceptions, frank disclosure must be reckoned one of the main principles of Gothic architecture.

FIG. 60.—DOORWAY FROM CHURCH AT BATALHA. (BEGUN 1385.)

Elaboration and simplicity were both so well known to the Gothic architect that it is difficult to say that either of these qualities belongs exclusively to his work. But he was rarely simple when he had the opportunity of being elaborate, and simplicity was perhaps rather forced upon him by the circumstances under which he worked, by rude materials, scanty funds, and lack of skilled workmen, than freely chosen. Many of the great works of the Gothic period are as elaborate as they could be made (Fig. 60), and yet, when simplicity had to be the order of the day, no architecture has lent it such a grace as Gothic.

The last pair of qualities is similarity and contrast. What has been said about repetition has anticipated the remarks called for by these qualities, so far as to point out that even where the arrangement of the building dictated the repetition of similar features, a general resemblance, and not an exact similarity, was considered sufficient. In the composition of masses of building, contrast and not similarity was the ruling principle. Even in the interiors of great churches which, as a rule, are far more regular than the exteriors, the contrast between the comparative plainness of the nave and the richness of the choir was an essential element of design.

External design in Gothic buildings depends almost entirely upon contrast for its power of charming the eye, and it is this circumstance which has left the successive generations of men who toiled at our great Gothic cathedrals so free to follow the bent of their own taste in their additions, rather than that of their forerunners.

But setting aside the irregularities due to the caprice of various builders, and the constant changes which took place in detail through the Gothic period, it is to contrast that we must trace most of the surprising effects attained by the architecture of the Middle Ages. The rich tracery was made richer by contrast with plain walls, the loftiest towers appeared higher from their contrast with the long level lines of roofs and parapets.

It is, in truth, one of the principal marks of the decadence which began in the fifteenth century that the principle of contrast was, to a considerable extent, abandoned, at least in the details of the buildings if not in their great masses. Walls were at that time panelled in imitation of the tracery of the adjoining windows, and no longer acted as a foil to them by their solid plainness; long rows of pinnacles, all exactly alike, followed the line of the parapets, and a repetition of absolutely identical features became the rule for the first time in the history of Gothic art.

There can be no doubt that had this modification run its natural course unchecked and undisturbed by the change in taste which abruptly brought the Gothic period to a close, it must have resulted in the deterioration of the art.

RENAISSANCE ARCHITECTURE.

CHAPTER X.

General View. Analysis of Buildings. Plans. Walls and Columns. Openings. Construction and Design

GOTHIC architecture had begun, before the close of the fifteenth century, to show marks of decadence, and men's minds and tastes were ripening for a change. The change, when it did take place, arose in Italy, and was a direct consequence of that burst of modern civilisation known as the revival of letters. All the characteristics of the middle ages were rapidly thrown off. The strain of old Roman blood in the modern Italians asserted itself, and almost at a bound, literature and the arts sprang back, like a bow unstrung, into the forms they had displayed fifteen hundred years before.

It became the rage to read the choice Greek and Latin authors, and to write Latin with a pedantic purity. Can we wonder that in painting, in sculpture, and in architecture, men reverted to the form, the style, and the decorations of the antique compositions, statues, and architectural remains? This was the more easy in Italy, as Gothic art had never at any time taken so firm a hold upon Italians as it had upon nations north of the Alps.

Though, however, the details and forms employed were all Roman, or Græco-Roman, they were applied to buildings essentially modern, and used with much freedom and spirit. This revival of classic taste in art is commonly and appropriately called Renaissance. In Italy it took place so rapidly that there was hardly any transition period. Brunelleschi, the first great Renaissance architect, began his work as early as the middle of the fifteenth century, and his buildings, in which classic details of great severity and purity are employed, struck, so to speak, a keynote which had been responded to all over Italy before the close of the fifteenth century.

To other countries the change spread later, and it found them less prepared to welcome it unreservedly. Accordingly, in France, in England, and in many parts of Germany, we find a transition period, during which buildings were designed in a mixed style. In England, the transition lasted almost through the sixteenth century.

As the century went on, a most picturesque and telling style, the earlier phases of which are known as Tudor and the later as Elizabethan, sprang up in England. It betrays in its mixture of Gothic and classic forms great incongruities and even monstrosities; but it allows unrestrained play for the fancies, and the best mansions and manors of the time, such as Hatfield, Hardwick, Burleigh, Bramshill, and Audley End, are unsurpassed in their picturesqueness and romantic charm.

The old red-brick, heavily chimneyed, and gabled buildings, with their large windows divided by bold mullions and transoms, and their simple noble outlines, are familiar to us all, and so are their characteristic features. The great hall with its oriel or its bay, the fine plastered ceiling, supported by heavy beams of timber; the wide oak staircase, with its carved balusters, and ornamented newel post, and heavy-moulded handrail; the old wainscoted parlour, with its magnificent chimney-piece reaching to the ceiling; these are all essentially English features, and are full of vigour and life, as indeed the work of every period of transition must almost necessarily prove.

The transitional period in France produced exquisite works more refined and elegantly treated than ours, but not so vigorous. Its manner is known as the François Premier (Francis I.) style. No modern buildings are more profusely ornamented, and yet not spoilt.

In Germany, the Castle of Heidelberg may be named as a well-known specimen of the transition period, a period over which however we must not linger. Suffice it to say, that sooner or later the change was fully accomplished in every European country, and Renaissance architecture, modified as climate, materials, habits, or even caprice suggested, yet the same in its essential characteristics, obtained a firm footing: this it has succeeded in retaining, though not to the exclusion of other styles, for now nearly three centuries.

In Italy, Renaissance churches, great and small—from St. Peter's downwards—and magnificent secular buildings, some, like the Vatican Palace or the Library of St. Mark at Venice, for public purposes, but most for the occupation of the great wealthy and princely families, abound in Naples, Rome, Florence, Genoa, Venice, Milan, and indeed every great city.

In France, the transition period was succeeded by a time when vast undertakings, *c.g.* the Hôtel de Ville, the Louvre, the Tuileries, Versailles, were carried out in the revived style with the utmost magnificence, and were imitated in every part of the country in the structures greater or smaller which were then built.

In England, the works of Inigo Jones, and of Wren, are the most famous works of the developed style, and to the last-named architect we owe a cathedral second to none in Europe for its beauty of outline, and play of light and shade. To Germany, and the countries of the north-east Europe, and to Spain and Portugal on the south, the style also extended with no very great modification, either of its general forms or of its details.

ANALYSIS OF BUILDINGS.

Plan.

The plan of Renaissance buildings was uniform and symmetrical, and the picturesqueness of the Gothic times was abandoned. The plans of churches were not widely different from those in use in Italy before the revival of classic art took place, but it will be remembered that these were by no means so irregular or picturesque at any time as the plans of French and English cathedral churches.

In secular architecture, the vast piles erected in the sixteenth and seventeenth centuries by Italian, French, and Spanish architects are to the last degree orderly in their disposition. They are adapted to a great variety of purposes, and they display a varying degree of skill. The palaces of Genoa are, on the one hand, among the cleverest examples of planning existing; on the other hand, many of the palaces in France are weak and poor to the last degree. As a rule the scale of the plan is more considerable than in Gothic work. A very large building is often not divided into more parts than a small one, or one of moderate size. In St. Peter's, for example, there are only four bays between the west front and the dome, everything being on a most gigantic scale. As a contrast to this principle we may cite the nave of the Gothic cathedral at Milan, which is not so long at St. Peter's, but has at least thrice as many bays, and looks much larger in consequence.

No style affords more room for skill in planning than the Renaissance, and in no style is the exercise of such skill more repaid by results.

Walls and Columns.

In the treatment of external walls, the mediæval use of small materials, involving many joints for the exterior of walls has quite disappeared, and they are universally faced with stone or plaster, and are consequently uniformly smooth. Perhaps the principal feature to note is the very great use made of that elaborate sort of masonry in which the joints of the stones are very carefully channelled or otherwise marked, and which is known by the singularly inappropriate name of rustic work. The basements of most Italian and French palaces are rusticated, and in many cases (as the Pitti Palace, Florence) rustic work covers an entire façade.

The Gothic mouldings in receding planes disappear entirely, and the classic architrave takes their place. The orders are again revived and are used (as the Romans often used them) as purely decorative features added for the mere sake of ornament to a wall sufficient without them, and are freely piled one upon the other. Palladio (a very influential Italian architect) reproduced the use of lofty pilasters running through two or even more storeys of the building, and often combined one tall order and two short ones in his treatment of the same part of the building, a contrivance which in less clever hands than his has given rise to the greatest confusion.

The Renaissance architects also revived the late Roman manner of employing the column and entablature. They frequently carried on the top of a column a little square pier divided up as the architrave and frieze proper to the column would be divided, and they surmounted it with a cornice which was carried quite round this pier, and from this curious compound pedestal an arch will frequently spring. The classic portico, with pediments, was constantly employed by them; and small pediments over window heads were common. A peculiarity worth mention is the introduction in many Italian palaces of a great crowning cornice, proportioned not to the size of the columns and of the order upon which it rests (if an order be employed), but to the height of the whole building. Much fine effect is obtained by means of this feature; it is, however, better fitted for sunny Italy than for gloomy England, and it is not an unmixed success when repeated in our climate.

Towers are less frequently employed than by the Gothic architects, and indeed in Italy the sky-line was less thought of at this period than it was in the middle ages. In churches, towers sometimes occur, nowhere more picturesque than those designed by Sir Christopher Wren for many of his London parish churches. The frequent use of the dome takes the place of the tower both in churches and secular buildings.

Openings.

Openings are both flat-headed and semicircular, occasionally elliptical, but hardly ever pointed. Renaissance buildings may be to some extent divided into those which depend for effect upon window openings, and those which depend chiefly upon architectural features such as cornices, pilasters, and orders. Among the buildings where fenestration (or the treatment of windows) is relied upon the palaces of Venice stand pre-eminent as compositions admirably designed for effect and very successful. In them the openings are massed near the centre of the façade, and strong piers are left near the angles, a simple expedient when once known, and one inherited from the Gothic palaces in that city, but giving remarkable individuality of character to this group of buildings.

In roofs, including vaults and domes, we meet with a divergence of practice between Italy and France. In Italy low-pitched roofs were the rule: the parapet alone often formed the sky-line, and the dome and pediment are usually the only telling features of the outline. France, on the other hand, revived a most picturesque feature of Gothic days, namely, the high-pitched roof, employing it in the shape commonly known as the Mansard[32] roof. Nothing adds more to the effectiveness of the great French Renaissance buildings than these lofty terminals.

The dome is, however, the glory of this style, as it had been of the Roman. It is the one feature by which revived and original classic architects retain a clear and defined advantage over Gothic architects, who, strange to say, all but abandoned the dome. The mouldings and other ornaments of the Renaissance are much the same as those of the Roman style, which the Italians revived; their sculptures and their mural decorations were all originally drawn from classic sources. These, however, attained very great excellence, and it is probable that such decorative paintings as Raphael and his scholars executed in Rome, at Genoa, at Mantua,

[32] Named after a French architect of the 17th century.

and elsewhere, far surpass anything which the old Roman decorative artists ever executed.

Construction and Design.

The earlier Renaissance buildings are remarkable for the great use which their architects made of carpentry, as the most modern structures are for the use of wrought and cast-iron construction. As regards carpentry, it is of course true that all the woodwork of the classic periods, and much of that done in the Gothic period, has perished, either through decay or fire; but making every allowance for this, we must still recognise a very great increase in the employment of timber as an integral part of large structures. Vaulted roofs for example are comparatively rare, and domes, even when the inner dome is of brickwork or masonry, have their outer envelope of carpentry. A disuse of brick and rough masonry, or rather a constant effort to conceal them from view, is a distinctive mark of Renaissance work. The Roman method of facing rough walls with fine stone was resorted to in the best buildings. In humbler buildings plaster is employed.

Renaissance architects made very free use of plaster. Inside and out this material is utilised, not merely to cover surfaces, but to form architectural features. Cornices, panels, and enrichments of all kinds modelled in plaster are constantly employed in the interior of rooms and buildings. On the exterior we constantly find imitations of similar architectural features proper to stone executed in plaster and simulating stone; a short-sighted practice which cannot be commended, and which has only cheapness and convenience in its favour. There can be no question of the fact that the features thus executed never equal those done in stone in their effectiveness, and are far more liable to decay.

Design in Renaissance buildings may be said to be directed towards producing a telling result by the effect of the buildings taken as a whole, rather than by the intricacy or the beauty of individual parts; and herein lies one of the great contrasts between Renaissance and Gothic architecture. A Renaissance building which fails to produce an impression as a whole is rarely felt to be successful. No better example of this can be given than the straggling, unsatisfactory Palace of Versailles, magnificent as it is in dimensions and rich in treatment. To the production of a homogeneous impression the arrangement of plan, the proportion of storeys, the contrasts of voids and solids, and above all the outline of the entire building, should be devoted.

The general arrangement of buildings is usually strictly symmetrical, one half corresponding to the other, and with some well-defined feature to mark the centre. Of course in very large buildings this does not occur, nor in the nature of things can it often take place in the sides of churches; but the individual features of such buildings, and all those parts of them which permit of symmetry in their arrangement, always display it.

Proportion plays an important part in the design of Renaissance buildings. The actual shape of openings, the proportion which they bear to voids, the proportion of storeys to one another; and, going into details, the proportions which the different features—*e.g.*, cornice, and the columns supporting it—should bear to one another, have to be carefully studied. It is to the possession of a keen sense of what makes a pleasing proportion and one satisfactory to the eye, that the great architects of Italy owed the greater part of their success.

Renaissance architecture is so familiar in its general features, and these have been so constantly repeated, that we may not easily recognise the great need for skill and taste which exists if they are to be designed so as to produce the most refined effect possible. Many of the successful buildings of the style owe their excellence to the great delicacy and elegance of the mode in which the details have been studied, rather than to the vigour and boldness with which the masses have been shaped and disposed; and though grandeur is the noblest quality of which the style is capable, yet many more opportunities for displaying grace and refinement than for attaining grandeur offer themselves, and by nothing are the best works of the style so well marked out as by the success with which those opportunities have been grasped and turned to account.

The concealment both of construction and arrangement is largely practised in Renaissance buildings. Behind an exterior wall filled by windows of uniform size and equally spaced, rooms large and small, corridors, staircases, and other features have to be provided for. This is completely in contrast to the Gothic principle of displaying frankly on the outside the arrangement of what is within; but it must be remembered that art often works most happily and successfully when limited by apparently strict and difficult conditions, and these rules have not prevented the great architects of the Renaissance from accomplishing works where both the exterior and the interior are thoroughly successful, and are brought into such happy harmony that the difficulties have clearly been no bar to success. There is no canon of art violated by such a method, the simple fact being that Gothic buildings are designed under one set of conditions and Renaissance under another.

It is less easy to defend the use of pilasters and columns large enough to appear as though they were the main support of the building, for purely decorative purposes; yet here perhaps the fault lies rather in the extent to which the practice has been carried, and above all the scale upon which it is carried out, than in anything else. Small columns are constantly employed in Gothic buildings in positions where they serve the æsthetic purpose of conveying a sense of support, but where it is impossible for them to carry any weight. The Renaissance architects have done the same thing on a large scale, but it must not be forgotten that they only revived a Roman practice as part of the ancient style to which they reverted, and that they are not responsible for originating it.

It will be understood therefore that symmetry, strict uniformity, not mere similarity, in features intended to correspond, and constant repetition, are leading principles in Renaissance architecture. These qualities tend to breadth rather than picturesqueness of effect, and to similarity rather than contrast. Simplicity and elaboration are both compatible with Renaissance design; the former distinguishes the earlier and purer examples of the style, the latter those more recent and more grandiose.

It should be observed that in the transition styles, such as our own Elizabethan, or the French style of Francis the First, these principles of design are mixed up in a very miscellaneous way with those followed in the Gothic period. The result is often puzzling and inconsistent if we attempt to analyse it with exactness, but rarely fails to charm by its picturesque and irregular vividness.

CHAPTER XI.

RENAISSANCE ARCHITECTURE IN ITALY.

Florence. Rome. Venice, Vicenza, Verona. Milan, Pavia. Genoa, Turin,
Naples. Country Villas

RENAISSANCE architecture—the architecture of the classic revival—had
its origin in Italy, and should be first studied in the land of its birth. There are
more ways than one in which it may be attempted to classify Italian Renaissance
buildings. The names of conspicuous architects are sometimes adopted for this
purpose, for now, for the first time, we meet with a complete record of the names
and performances of all architects of note: the men who raised the great works of
Gothic art are, with a few exceptions, absolutely unknown to us. An approximate
division into three stages can also be recognised. There is an early, a developed,
and a late Renaissance, but this is very far indeed from being a completely marked
series, and was more interfered with by local circumstances and by the character
and genius of individual artists than in Gothic. For this reason a local division will
be of most service. The best examples exist in the great cities, with a few exceptions, and it is almost more useful to group them—as the paintings of the Renaissance are also often grouped—by locality than in either of the other methods.

FLORENCE.

Renaissance architecture first sprang into existence in Florence. Here chiefly
the works of the early Renaissance are met with, and the names of the great Florentine architects are Brunelleschi and Alberti.

Brunelleschi was a citizen of Florence, of very ardent temperament and great
energy, and a true artist. He was born in 1377, was originally trained as a gold-

smith and sculptor, but devoted himself to the study of architecture, and early set his heart upon being appointed to complete the dome of the then unfinished cathedral of Florence, of which some account has already been given.

Florence in the fifteenth century was full of artistic life, and the revival of learning and arts had then begun to take definite shape. The first years of the century found Brunelleschi studying antiquities at Rome, to fit himself for the work he desired to undertake. After his return to his native city, he ultimately succeeded in the object of his ambition; the cathedral was entrusted to him, and he erected the large pointed dome with which it is crowned. He also erected two large churches in Florence, which, as probably the first important buildings designed and built in the new style, possess great interest. Santo Spirito, one of these, shows a fully matured system of architectural treatment, and though it is quite true that it was a revived system, yet the application of it to a modern building, different in its purpose and in its design from anything the Romans had ever done, is little short of a work of genius.

Santo Spirito has a very simple and beautifully regular plan, and its interior has a singular charm and grace: over the crossing is raised a low dome. The columns of the arcade are Corinthian columns, and the refinement of their detail and proportions strikes the eye at once on entering the building. The influence of Brunelleschi, who died in 1440, was perpetuated by the works and writings of Alberti (born 1398) an architect of literary cultivation who wrote a systematic treatise which became extremely popular, and helped to form the taste and guide the practice of his contemporaries. He lived till near the close of the fifteenth century, and erected some buildings of great merit. To Alberti we owe the design of the Ruccellai Palace in Florence, a building begun in 1460, and which had been preceded by somewhat bolder and simpler designs. This is a three storey building, but has pilasters carried up the piers between the windows and a regular entablature and cornice[33] at each storey. The building is elegant and graceful, and though the employment of the orders[34] as its decoration gives it a distinctive character, it bears a strong general resemblance to the group of which the Strozzi Palace (Fig. 61) may be taken as the type.

The earliest Florentine palaces are the Riccardi, which dates from 1430, and the Pitti of almost the same date; Brunelleschi is said to have been consulted in the design of both, but Michelozzo was the architect. The distinguishing characteristic of the early palaces in this city is solidity, which rises from the fact that they were also fortresses. The Pitti, well known for its picture gallery, is a building of vast extent, built throughout in very boldly rusticated masonry, the joints and projections of the stones being greatly exaggerated. The Riccardi, a square block of building, bears a considerable resemblance to the Strozzi, but is plainer. It is a most dignified building in its effect.

[33] An entablature is the superstructure which ordinarily is carried by a column, and which it is usual to divide into architrave (or beam), frieze, and cornice.

[34] An order consists of a column (or pilaster) with its distinctive base and capital, its entablature, and the appropriate decorations. There are five orders, differing in proportions, in the degree of enrichment required, and in the design of the base and capital of the column or pilaster, and of the entablature.

The Strozzi Palace (Fig. 61) was the next great palatial pile erected. It was designed by Cronaca, and begun in 1498. Like the Riccardi, it is of three storeys, with a bold projecting cornice. The whole wall is covered with rusticated masonry; the windows of the lower floor are small and square; those of the two upper floors are larger and semicircular headed, and with a shaft acting as a mullion, and carrying arches which occupy the window head with something like tracery. The entrance is by a semicircular headed archway. There is a great height of unpierced wall in the lowest storey and above the heads of the two upper ranges of windows; and to this and the bold overhanging cornice, this building, and those like it, owe much of their dignity and impressiveness. An elevation, such as our illustration, may convey a fair idea of the good proportion and ensemble of the front, but it is difficult without actually seeing the buildings to appreciate the effect produced by such palaces as these, seen foreshortened in the narrow streets, and with the shadows from their bold cornices and well-defined openings intensified by the effect of the Italian sun.

FIG. 61.—STROZZI PALACE AT FLORENCE. (BEGUN 1489.)

Many excellent palatial buildings belong to the end of the fifteenth century. One among them is attributed to Bramante (who died 1513), a Florentine, whom we shall meet with in Rome and elsewhere. The Guadagni Palace has an upper storey entirely open, forming a sheltered loggia, but it is mentioned here chiefly on account of the decorations incised on its walls by the method known as Sgraffito. Part of the plain wall is covered in this way with decorative designs, which appear as though drawn with a bold line on their surface. An example of this decoration will be found in our illustration (Fig. 62), representing a portion of the Loggia del

Consiglio at Verona.

The series of great Florentine palaces closes with a charming example, the Pandolfini, designed by the great Raphael, and commenced in 1520—in other words, in the first quarter of the sixteenth century.

This palace is only one of many instances to be found in Italy of the skill in more walks of art than one, of some of the greatest artists. Raphael, though best known as a painter, executed works of sculpture of great merit, and designed some other buildings besides the one now under notice. The Pandolfini Palace (Fig. 63) is small, the main building having only four windows in the front and two storeys in height, with a low one-storey side building. Its general design has been very successfully copied in the Travellers' Club House, Pall Mall. On comparing this with any of the previously named designs, it will be seen that the semicircular headed windows have disappeared, the rusticated masonry is only now retained at the angles, and to emphasise the side entrance; and a small order with a little pediment (*i.e.* gable) is employed to mark each opening, door or window. In short this building belongs not only to another century, but to that advanced school of art to which we have given the name of developed Italian Renaissance.

FIG. 62.—PART OF THE LOGGIA DEL CONSIGLIO AT VERONA.

(16th Century.) Showing the incised decoration known as Sgraffito.

In Florence some of the work of Michelangelo is to be met with. His own house is here; so is the famous Medici chapel, a work in which we find him displaying power at once as a sculptor and an architect. This interior is very fine and very studied both in its proportions and its details. The church of the Annunziata, remarkable for a fine dome, carried on a drum resting directly on the ground, is the foremost Renaissance church in Florence.

The contrast between early and matured Renaissance can indeed be better recognised in Florence than in almost any other city. The early work, that of Bramante, Brunelleschi, and the architects who drew their inspirations from these masters, was delicate and refined. The detail was always elegant, the ornament always unobtrusive, and often most graceful. Features comparatively small in scale were employed, and were set off by the use of plain wall-surface, which was unhesitatingly displayed. The classic orders were used in a restricted, unobtrusive way, and with pilasters in preference to columns; and though probably the architects themselves would have repudiated the idea that the Gothic art, which they had cast behind them, influenced their practice of revived classic in the remotest degree, it is nevertheless true that many of these peculiarities, and still more the general quality of the designs, were to a large extent those to which the practice of Gothic architecture had led them.

A change which was partly due to a natural desire for progress, was helped on by the great attention paid by students of architecture to the remains of ancient Roman buildings; but it was the influence excited by the powerful genius of Michelangelo, and by the gigantic scale and vigorous treatment of his masterpiece, St. Peter's, which was the proximate occasion of a revolution in taste and practice, to which, the labours, both literary and artistic, of Vignola, and the designs of Palladio, gave form and consistency. In the fully-developed, or, as it is sometimes called, pure Renaissance of Italy, great use is made of the classic orders and pediment, and indeed of all the features which the Romans had employed. Plain wall space almost disappears under the various architectural features introduced, and all ornaments, details, and mouldings become bolder and richer, but often less refined and correct in design.

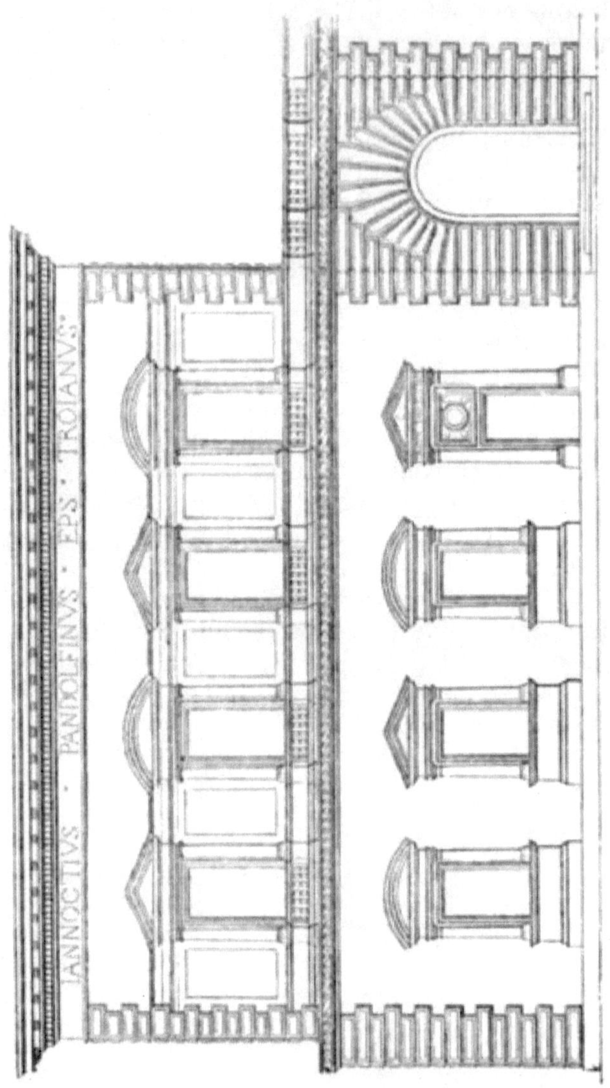

FIG. 63.—THE PANDOLFINI PALACE, FLORENCE. DESIGNED BY
RAPHAEL.

(Begun 1520.)

ROME.

Rome, the capital of the country, contains, as was fit, the central building of
the fully-developed Renaissance, St. Peter's. Bramante, the Florentine, was the architect to whom the task of designing a cathedral to surpass anything existing in
Europe was committed by Pope Julius II. at the opening of the sixteenth century.
Some such project had been entertained, and even begun, fifty years earlier, but

the enterprise was now started afresh, a new design was made, and the first stone was laid by the Pope in 1506. Bramante died in some six or seven years, and five or six architects in succession, one of whom was Raphael, proceeded with the work, without advancing it rapidly, for nearly half a century, during which time the design was modified again and again. In 1546 the great Michelangelo was appointed architect, and the last eighteen years of his life were spent in carrying on this great work. He completed the magnificent dome in all its essential parts, and left the church a Greek cross (*i.e.* one which has all its four arms equal) on plan, with the dome at the crossing. The boast is attributed to him that he would take the dome of the Pantheon and hang it in the air; and this he has virtually accomplished in the dome of St. Peter's—a work of the greatest beauty of design and boldness of construction.

Unfortunately, at the beginning of the seventeenth century, Maderno was employed to lengthen the nave. This transformed the plan of the cathedral into a Latin cross. The existing portico was built at the same time; and in 1661 Bernini added the vast forecourt, lined by colonnades, which now forms the approach.

This cathedral, of which the history has been briefly sketched, is the largest in the world. As we now see it, it consists of a vast vestibule; a nave of four bays with side aisles; a vast square central space over which hangs the great dome; transepts and a choir, each of one bay and an apse. Outside the great central space, an aisle, not quite like the ordinary aisle of a church, exists, and there are two side chapels. It can be well understood that if the largest church in Christendom is divided into so few parts, these must be themselves of colossal dimensions, and the truth is that the piers are masses of masonry which can be called nothing else than vast, while the spaces spanned by the arches and vaults are prodigious. There is little sense of mystery about the interior of the building (Fig. 64), the eye soon grasps it as a whole, and hours must be spent in it before an idea of its gigantic size is at all taken in. The beauty of the colouring adds wonderfully to the effect of St. Peter's upon the spectator, for the walls are rich with mosaics and coloured marbles; and the interior, the dome especially, with the drum upon which it rests, are decorated in colour throughout, with fine effect and in excellent taste. The interior is amply lighted, and, though very rich, not over decorated; its design is simple and noble in the extreme, and all its parts are wonderful in their harmony. The connection between the dome and the rest of the building is admirable, and there is a sense of vast space when the spectator stands under that soaring vault which belongs to no other building in the world.

The exterior is disappointing as long as the building is seen in front, for the façade is so lofty and advances so far forward as to cut off the view of the lower part of the dome. To have an idea of the building as Michelangelo designed it, it is necessary to go round to the back; and then, with the height of the drum fully seen and the contour of the dome, with all its massy lines of living force, carrying the eye with them right up to the elegant lantern that crowns the summit, some conception of the hugeness and the symmetry of this mountain of art seems to dawn on the mind. But even here it is with the utmost difficulty that one can apply any scale to the mass, so that the idea which the mind forms of its bulk is continually fluctuating.

The history of this building extends over all the period of developed Renaissance in Rome, and its list of architects includes all the best known names. By the side of it every other church, even St. John Lateran, appears insignificant; so that the secular buildings in Rome, which are numerous, and some of them excellent, are more worth attention than the churches, though not a few of the three hundred churches and basilicas of the metropolis of Italy are good examples of Renaissance.

FIG. 64.—ST. PETER'S AT ROME. INTERIOR. (1506-1661.)

The altars, tombs, and other architectural or semi-architectural works which occur in many of the churches of Rome, are, however, finer works of art as a rule than the buildings which they adorn. Such gems are not confined to Rome, but are to be found throughout Italy: many of them belong to the best period of art. Marble is generally the material, and the light as a rule falls on these works in one direction only. Under these circumstances the most subtle moulding gives a play of light and shade, and the most delicate carving produces a richness of effect which cannot be attained in exterior architecture, executed for the most part in stone, exposed to the weather, and seen by diffused and reflected light. Nothing of this sort is finer than the monuments by Sansovino, erected in Sta. Maria del Popolo at Rome, one of which we illustrate on a small scale (Fig. 65). The magnificent altar-piece in Sta. Coronale at Vicenza, in which is framed Bellini's picture of the baptism of Christ, is another example, on an unusually large scale—fine in style, and covered with beautiful ornament.

No secular building exists in Rome so early or so simple as the severe Florentine palaces; but Bramante, who belongs to the early period, erected there the fine Cancelleria palace; and the Palazzo Giraud (Fig. 66). These buildings resemble one another very closely; each bears the impress of refined taste, but delicacy has been carried almost to timidity. The pilasters and cornices which are employed have the very slightest projection, but the large mass of the wall as compared with the openings, secures an appearance of solidity, and hence of dignity. The interior of the Cancelleria contains an arcaded quadrangle (*cortile*) of great beauty. Smaller palaces belonging to the same period and of the same refined, but somewhat weak, character exist in Rome.

FIG. 65.—MONUMENT, BY SANSOVINO, IN STA. MARIA DEL POPOLO, ROME.

(15th Century.)

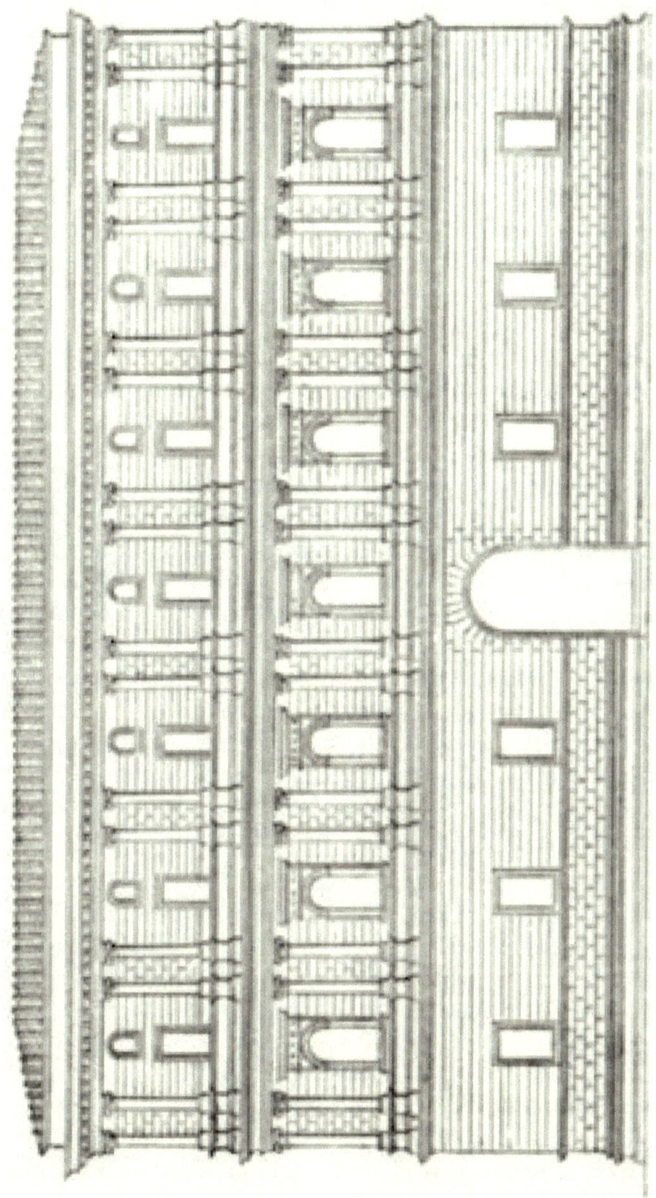

FIG. 66.—PALAZZO GIRAUD (NOW TORLONIA), ROME. BY BRA-MANTE. (1506.)

The Vatican Palace is so vast that, like St. Peter's, it took more than one generation to complete. To Bramante's time belongs the great Belvedere, since much altered, but in its original state an admirable work. This palace also can show some remarkable additions by Bernini, a much later architect, with much that is not admirable or remarkable by other hands. The finest Roman palace is the Farnese, begun by San Gallo in 1530, continued by Michelangelo, and completed by Giacomo della Porta, each architect having altered the design. This building, notwithstanding its chequered history, is a dignified, impressive mass. It has only three storeys and a scarcely marked basement, and is nearly square, with a large quadrangle in its heart. It is very lofty, and has a great height of unpierced wall over each storey of windows, and is crowned by a bold and highly-enriched cornice—an unusual thing for Rome. In this, and in many palaces built about the same time, the windows are ornamented in the same manner as those of the Pandolfini Palace at Florence; the use of pilasters instead of columns is general; the openings are usually square-headed, circular heads being usually confined to arcades and loggie; the angles are marked by rustication, and the only cornice is the one that crowns the whole. This general character will apply to most of the works of Baldassare Peruzzi, Vignola, Sangallo, and Raphael, who were, with Michelangelo, the foremost architects in Rome in the sixteenth century. But "the works executed by Michelangelo are in a bolder and more pictorial style, as are also many productions grafted on the earlier Italian manner by a numerous class of succeeding architects. In these is to be remarked a greater use of columns, engaged and isolated; stronger but less studied details; and a greater use of colonnades, in which however the combination with the semicircular arch is still unusual, the antique in this respect being followed to a great disadvantage. Still there is a nobility, a palatial look about these large mansions which is very admirable, and is to be remarked in all the palaces, even up to the time of Borromini, *circa* 1640, by whom all the principles and parts of Roman architecture were literally turned topsy-turvey. Michelangelo's peculiar style was more thoroughly carried out on ecclesiastical buildings, and as practised by his successors, exhibits much that is fine, in large masses, boldly projecting cornices, three-quarter columns, and noble domes; but it is otherwise debased by great misconceptions as to the reasonable application of architecture."—M. D. W.

In the seventeenth century a decline set in. The late Renaissance has neither the severity of the early, nor the dignified richness of the mature time, but is extravagant; though at Rome examples of its extreme phase are not common. Maderno, who erected the west front of St. Peter's, and Bernini, who added the outer forecourt and also built the curiously designed state staircase (the *scala regia*) in the Vatican, are the foremost architects. To these must be added Borromini. The great Barberini Palace belongs to this century; but perhaps its most characteristic works are the fountains, some of them with elaborate architectural backgrounds, which ornament many of the open places in Rome. Few of the buildings of the eighteenth century in Rome, or indeed in Italy generally, claim attention as architectural works of a high order of merit.

Before leaving central Italy for the north, it is necessary to mention the masterpiece of Vignola—the great Farnese Palace at Caprarola; and to add that in every city of importance examples more or less admirable of the art of the time were erected.

VENICE, VICENZA, AND VERONA.

The next great group of Renaissance buildings is to be found at Venice, where the style was adopted with some reluctance, and not till far on in the sixteenth century. At first we meet with some admixture of Gothic elements; as, for example, in the rebuilding of the internal quadrangle of the Ducal Palace. Pointed arches are partly employed in this work, which was completed about the middle of the sixteenth century. In the earlier palaces—which, it will be remembered, are comparatively narrow buildings standing side by side on the banks of the canals—the storeys are well marked; the windows are round headed with smaller arches within the main ones; the orders when introduced are kept subordinate; the windows are grouped together in the central portion of the front, as was the case with those of the Gothic palaces, and very little use is made of rusticated masonry. The Vendramini, Cornaro, and Trevisano Palaces conform to this type. To the same period belong one or two fine churches, the most famous being San Zacaria, a building with a very delicately panelled front, and a semicircular pediment in lieu of a gable; here, too, semicircular-headed openings are made use of. In many of these churches and other buildings, a beautiful ornament, which may be regarded as typical of early Venetian Renaissance, is to be found. It is the shell ornament, so called from its resemblance to a flat semicircular shell, ribbed from the centre to the circumference (Fig. 67).

FIG. 67.—ITALIAN SHELL ORNAMENT.

As time went on the style was matured into one of great richness, not to say ostentation, with which the names of Sansovino, Sanmichele, Palladio, and Scamozzi are identified as the prominent architects of the latter part of the sixteenth and seventeenth centuries. In this city of palaces Sansovino, also a very fine sculptor, built the celebrated Library of St. Mark, facing the Ducal Palace, which has been followed very closely in the design of the Carlton Club, Pall Mall. Here, as in the splendid Cornaro Palace, the architect relied chiefly upon the columns and entablatures of the orders, combined with grand arcades enriched by sculpture, so arranged as to occupy the spaces between the columns; almost the whole of the wall-space was so taken up, and the basement only was covered with rustication, often rough worked, as at the beautiful Palazzo Pompeii, Verona, and the Grimani Palace, Venice.

"Sanmichele's works are characterised chiefly by their excellent proportions, their carefully studied detail, their strength, and their beauty (qualities so difficult to combine). We believe that the buildings of this great architect and engineer at Verona are pre-eminent in their peculiar style over those of any other artist of the sixteenth century. In a different, but no less meritorious, manner are the buildings designed by Sansovino; they are characterised by a more sculptural and ornamental character; order over order with large arched voids in the interspaces of the columns producing a pictorial effect which might have led his less gifted followers into a false style, but for the example of the celebrated Palladio." —M. D. W.

To the latest time of the Renaissance in Venice belongs the picturesque domed church of St. Maria della Salute, conspicuous in many views of the Grand Canal, a building which is a work of real genius in spite of what is considered its false taste. It dates from 1632. The architect is Longhena.

FIG. 68.—THE CHURCH OF THE REDENTORE, VENICE. (1576.)

An almost endless series of palaces and houses can be found in Venice, all of them rich, but few of great extent, for every foot of space had to be won from the sea by laborious engineering. There are some features which never fail to present themselves, and which are consequences of the conditions under which the structures were designed. All rise from the water, and require to admit of gondolas coming under the walls; hence there is always a principal central entrance with steps in front, but this entrance never has any sort of projecting portico or porch, and is never very much larger than the other openings in the front. As a straight frontage to the water had to be preserved, we hardly ever meet with such a thing as a break or projection of any sort; but the Venetian architects have found other means of giving interest to their elevations, and it is to the very restrictions imposed by circumstances that we owe the great originality displayed in their earlier buildings. The churches do not usually front directly on to the water; and though they are almost all good of their kind, they are far more commonplace than the palaces. The system of giving variety to the façade of the secular buildings by massing openings near the centre, has been already referred to. Both shadow and richness were also aimed at in the employment of projecting balconies; in fact the two usually go together, for the great central window or group of windows mostly has a large and rich balcony belonging to it.

Not far from Venice is Vicenza, and here Palladio, whose best buildings in Venice are churches, such, for example, as the Redentore (Fig. 68), enjoyed an opportunity of erecting a whole group of palaces, the fronts of which are extremely remarkable as designs; though, being executed in brick and plastered, they are now falling to ruin. There is much variety in them, and while some of them rely upon his device of lofty pilasters to include two storeys of the building under one storey of architectural treatment, others are handled differently. In all a singularly fine feeling for proportion and for the appropriate omission as well as introduction of ornament is to be detected. The worst defect of these fronts is, however, that they appear more like masks than the exteriors of buildings, for there is little obvious connection between the features of the exterior and anything which we may suppose to exist inside the building. The finest architectural work left behind by Palladio in this city are, however, the great arcades with which he surrounded the Basilica, a vast building of the middle ages already alluded to. These arcades are two storeys high, and are rich, yet vigorous; they ornament the great structure, the roof of which may be seen rising behind, without overpowering it.

MILAN AND PAVIA.

In Milan two buildings at least belong to the early Renaissance. These are the sacristy of Sta. Maria presso San Satiro, and the eastern portion of the church of Sta. Maria delle Grazie; Bramante was the architect of both. The last-named work is an addition to an existing Gothic church; it is executed in the terra-cotta and brick of Lombardy, materials which the Renaissance architects seemed to shun in later times, and is full of the most profuse and elegant ornaments. The design consists of a dome, treated externally a little like some of the Lombard domes of earlier date; and three apses forming choir and transepts. It is divided into several stages, and abundantly varied in its panelling and arcading, and is full of vigour. By Bramante is also the very beautiful arcaded quadrangle of the great hospital at Milan, the Gothic front of which has been already noticed. There are many Renaissance buildings of later date in Milan, but none very remarkable.

FIG. 69.—THE CERTOSA NEAR PAVIA. PART OF THE WEST
FRONT. (BEGUN BY BORGOGNONE 1473.)

To the early period belongs the design of the façade of the Certosa near Pavia,
part of which is shown (Fig. 69). This was begun as early as 1473, by Ambrogio
Borgognone, and was long in hand. It proceeded on the lines settled thus early,
and is probably the richest façade belonging to any church in Christendom; it is
executed entirely in marble. Sculpture is employed to adorn every part that is near
the eye, and especially the portal, which is flanked by pilasters with their faces

panelled and occupied by splendid *alti relievi*. The upper part is enriched by inlays of costly marbles, but the two systems of decoration do not thoroughly harmonise; for the upper half looks coarse, which it in reality is not, in contrast with the delicate richness of the carving near the eye. The great features, such as the entrance, the windows, and the angle pinnacles are thoroughly good, and an arcade of small arches is twice introduced,—once running completely across the front at about half its height, and again near the top of the central portion,—with excellent effect (see Frontispiece).

GENOA, TURIN, AND NAPLES.

Turning now to Genoa we find, as we may in several great cities of Italy, that very great success has been achieved by an artist whose works are to be seen in no other city, and whose fame is proportionally restricted. Just as the power of Luini as a painter can only be fully understood at Milan, or that of Giulio Romano at Mantua, so the genius of Alessio (1500 to 1572) as an architect can only be understood at Genoa. From the designs of this architect were built a series of well planned and imposing palaces. These buildings have most of them the advantage of fine and roomy sites. The fronts are varied, but as a rule consist of a very bold basement, with admirably-treated vigorous mouldings, supporting a lighter superstructure, and in one or two instances flanked by an open arcade at the wings. The entrance gives access, through a vaulted hall, to the cortile, which is usually planned and designed in the most effective manner; and in several instances the state staircase is so combined with this feature that on ascending the first flight the visitor comes to a point of sight for which the whole may be said to have been designed, and from which a splendid composition of columns and arches is seen. The rooms and galleries in these palaces are very fine, and in several instances have been beautifully decorated in fresco by Perino del Vaga.

Alessio was also the architect of a large domical church (il Carignano) in the same city; but it is far inferior in merit to his series of palaces. Genoa also possesses a famous church (the Annunziata) of late Renaissance, attributed to Puget (1622-1694). It is vaulted, and enriched with marbles, mosaics, and colour to such an extent that it may fairly claim to be the most gaudy church in Italy, which is unfortunate, as its original undecorated design is fine and simple.

Turin in the north, and Naples in the south, are chiefly remarkable for examples of the latest and more or less debased Renaissance, and we therefore do not propose to illustrate or describe any of the buildings in either city.

COUNTRY VILLAS.

FIG. 70.—VILLA MEDICI—ON THE PINCIAN HILL NEAR ROME. BY ANNIBALE LIPPI

(NOW THE *Académie Française*). (A.D. 1540.)

As the ancient Roman patrician had his villa, which was his country resort, the Italian of the revival followed his example, and, if he was wealthy enough, built himself a pleasure house, which he called a villa, either in the immediate suburbs of his city, or at some little distance away in the country. These buildings occur throughout Italy. Many of them are excellent examples of Renaissance architecture of a more modest type than that of the palaces. The Villa Papa Giulio, built from the designs of Vignola, and the Villa Medici, designed by Annibale Lippi, but attributed, for some unknown reason, to Michelangelo, may be mentioned as among the most thoroughly architectural out of some twenty or more splendid villas in the suburbs of Rome alone. Many of these buildings were erected late in the Renaissance period, and are better worth attention for their fine decorations and the many works of art collected within their walls than as architectural studies—but this is not always the case; and as they were mostly designed to serve the purpose of elegant museums rather than that of country houses as we understand the term, they usually possess noble interiors, and exhibit throughout elaborate finish, choice materials, and lavish outlay.

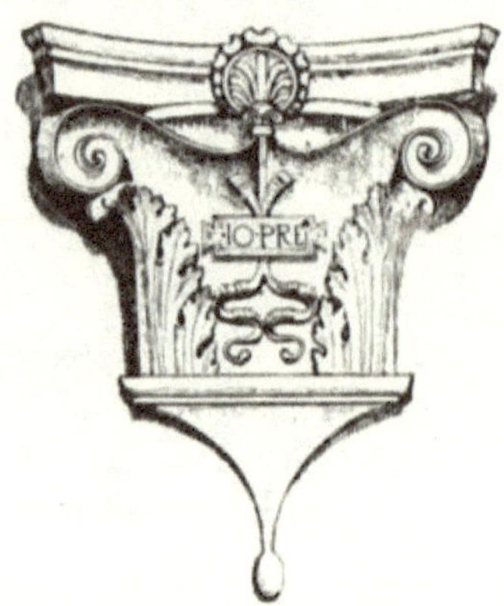

FIG. 70A.—EARLY RENAISSANCE CORBEL

CHAPTER XII.

RENAISSANCE ARCHITECTURE IN FRANCE AND NORTHERN EUROPE.

CHRONOLOGICAL SKETCH.

1. France. Chronological Sketch

THE revived classic architecture came direct from Italy, and did not reach France till it had been well established in the land of its origin. It was not however received with the same welcome which hailed its appearance in Italy. Gothic architecture had a strong hold on France, and accordingly, instead of a sudden change, we meet with a period of transition, during which buildings were erected with features partly Gothic and partly Renaissance, and on varied principles of design.

French Renaissance underwent great fluctuations, and it is less easy to divide it into broad periods than to refer, as most French writers prefer to do, to the work of each prominent monarch's reign separately.

Francis the First (1515-1547) made the architecture of Italy fashionable in his kingdom, and his name is borne by the beautiful transitional style of his day. This in most cases retains some Gothic forms, and the principles of composition are in the main Gothic, but the features are mostly of Italian origin, though handled with a fineness of detail and a smallness of scale that is not often met with, even in early Italian Renaissance. There are few buildings more charming in the architecture of any age or country than the best specimens of the style of Francis the First, and none that can bear so much decoration and yet remain so little overladen by the ornaments they carry. The finest example is the Château of Chambord, a large building, nearly square on plan, with round corner towers, capped by simple and very steep roofs, at the angles; and having as its central feature, a large and lofty mass of towers, windows and arcades, surmounted by steep roofs, ending in a kind of huge lantern. The windows have mullions and transoms like Gothic windows, but pilasters of elegant Renaissance design ornament the walls. The main cornice is a kind of compromise between an Italian and a Gothic treatment. Dormer windows, high and sharply pointed, but with little pilasters and pediments as their ornaments, occur constantly; and the chimneys, which are of immense mass and great height, are panelled profusely, and almost ostentatiously displayed, especially on the central portion. In the interior of the central building is a famous staircase; but the main attractions are the bright and animated appearance of the whole exterior, and the richness and gracefulness of the details.

The same architecture is to be well seen in the north side of the famous Château of Blois—a building parts of which were executed in three different periods of French architecture. The exterior of the *François premier* part of Blois is irregular, and portions of the design are wildly picturesque; on the side which fronts towards the quadrangle, the architecture is more symmetrically designed, and beauty rather than picturesque effect has been aimed at. An open staircase is the part of the quadrangle upon which most care has been lavished. Throughout the whole block of buildings the character of each individual feature and of every combination of features is graceful and *piquant*. The elegance and delicacy of some of the carved decoration in the interior is unsurpassed.

FIG. 71.—WINDOW FROM A HOUSE AT ORLEANS. (EARLY 16TH CENTURY.)

In the valley of the Loire there exist many noblemen's châteaux of this date, corresponding in general character with Chambord and Blois, though on a smaller scale. Of these Chénonceaux, fortunate alike in its design and its situation, is the most elegant and the best known: yet many others exist which approach it closely, such, for example, as the Château de Gaillon—a fragment of which forms part of the École des Beaux Arts at Paris—the Hôtel de Ville of Beaugency, the Châteaux of Châteaudun, Azay-le-Rideau, La Cote, and Ussé; the Hôtel d'Anjou at Angers, and the house of Agnes Sorel at Orleans.

In the streets of Orleans houses of this date (Fig. 71) are to be found, show-ing the style cleverly adapted to the requirements of town dwellings and shops. Several of them also possess courtyards with arcades or other architectural fea-tures treated with great freedom and beauty, for instance, the arcades in the house of *François Premier* (Fig. 72). An arcade in the courtyard of the Gothic Hôtel de Bourgtherould at Rouen, is one of the best known examples of the style remaining, and instances of it may be met with as far apart as at Caen (east end of church of St. Pierre) and Toulouse (parts of St. Sernin).

One Paris church, that of St. Eustache, belonging to this transitional period claims mention, since for boldness and completeness it is one of the best of any date in that city. St. Eustache is a five-aisled church with an apse, transept, and lateral chapels outside the outer aisle. It is vaulted throughout, and its plan and structure are those of a Gothic church in all respects. Its details are however all Re-naissance, but not so good as those to be found at Blois, nor so appropriately used, yet notwithstanding this it has a singularly impressive interior.

FIG. 72.—CAPITAL FROM THE HOUSE OF FRANCIS I., ORLEANS.
(1540.)

Meantime, and alongside the buildings resulting from this fusion of styles, others which were almost direct importations from Italy were rising; in some cases, if not in all, under the direction of Italian architects. Thus on Fontainebleau, which Francis I. erected, three or four Italian architects, one of whom was Vignola, were engaged. It may or may not have been this connection of the great architect with this work which gave him influence in France, but certainly almost the whole of the later French Renaissance, or at any rate its good time, was marked by a conformity to the practice of Vignola, in whose designs we usually find one order of columns or pilasters for each storey, rather than to that of Palladio, whose use of tall columns equalling in height two or more floors of the building has been already noticed.

Designs for the Louvre, the rebuilding of which was commenced in the reign of Francis the First (about A.D. 1544), were made by Serlio, an Italian; and though Pierre Lescot was the architect of the portion built in that reign, it is probable that the design obtained from Serlio was in the main followed. The part then finished, which, to a certain extent gave the keynote to the whole of this vast building, was unquestionably a happy effort, and may be taken to mark the establishment of a French version of matured Renaissance architecture. The main building has two orders of pilasters with cornices, &c., and above them a low attic storey, with short piers: at the angles a taller pavilion was introduced, and next the quadrangle arcades are introduced between the pilasters. The sculpture, some of it at least, is from the chisel of Jean Goujon; it is good and well placed, and the whole has an air of dignity and richness. The *Pavillon Richelieu*, shewn in our engraving (Fig. 73), was not built till the next century. The colossal figures are by Barye.

A little later in date than the early part of the Louvre was the Hôtel de Ville, built from the designs of Pietro da Cortona, an Italian, and said to have been begun in 1549. The building had been greatly extended before its recent total destruction by fire, but the central part, which was the original portion, was a fine vigorous composition, having two lofty pavilions, with high roofs at the extremities, and a remarkably rich stone lantern of great height for a central feature.

FIG. 73.—PAVILLON RICHELIEU OF THE LOUVRE, PARIS.

In the reign of Charles IX. the Palace of the Tuileries was commenced (1564) for Catherine de Médicis, from the designs of Philibert Delorme. Of this building, that part only which fronted the garden was erected at the time. Our illustration

(Fig. 74) shows the architectural character of a portion of it, and it is easy to detect that considerable alterations have by this time been introduced into the treatment of the features of Renaissance architecture. The bands of rustication passing round the pilasters as well as the walls, the broken pediments on the upper storey, surmounted by figures, and supported by long carved pilasters, and the shape of the dormer windows are all of them quite foreign to Renaissance architecture as practised in Italy, and may be looked upon as essentially French features. Similar details were employed in the work executed at about the same period, by the same and other architects, in other buildings, as may be seen by our illustration (Fig. 75) of a portion of Delorme's work at the Louvre. In these features, which may be found in the Château d'Anet and other works of the same time, and in the style to which they belong, may be seen the direct result of Michelangelo's Medici Chapel at Florence, a work which had much more effect on French than on Italian architecture. The full development of the architecture of Michelangelo (or rather the ornamental portions of it) is to be found in French Renaissance, rather than in the works of his own successors in Italy.

Much of the late sixteenth century architecture of France was very inferior, and the parts of the Louvre and Tuileries which date from the reign of Henry IV. are the least satisfactory portions of those vast piles.

FIG. 74.—PART OF THE TUILERIES, PARIS. (BEGUN 1564.)

Dating from the early part of the seventeenth century, we have the Palais Royal built for Richelieu, and the Palace of the Luxembourg, a building perhaps more correct and quiet than original or beautiful, but against which the reproach of extravagant ornament cannot certainly be brought.

FIG. 75.—CAPITAL FROM DELORME'S WORK AT THE LOUVRE.

(Middle of 16th Century.)

With Louis the Fourteenth (1643 to 1715) came in a great building period, of which the most striking memorial is the vast and uninteresting Palace of Versailles. The architect was the younger Mansard (1647 to 1768), and the vastness of the scale upon which he worked only makes his failure to rise to his grand opportunity the more conspicuous. The absence of features to diversify the sky-line is one of the greatest defects of this building, a defect the less excusable as the high-pitched roof of Gothic origin had never been abandoned in France. This roof has been employed with great success in many buildings of the French Renaissance. Apart from this fault, the architectural features of Versailles are so monotonous, weak, and uninteresting that the building, though its size may astonish the spectator, seldom rouses admiration.

Far better is the eastern block of the Louvre (the portion facing the Place du

Louvre), though here also we find the absence of high roofs, and the consequent monotony of the sky-line—a defect attaching to hardly any other portion of the building. Bernini was invited from Italy for this work, and there is a curious story in one of Sir Christopher Wren's published letters of an interview he had with Bernini while the latter was in Paris on this business, and of the glimpse which he was allowed to enjoy of the design the Italian had made. The building was, however, after all, designed and carried out by Perrault, and, though somewhat severe, possesses great beauty and much of that dignity in which Versailles is wanting.

The best French work of this epoch to be found in or out of Paris is probably the Hôtel des Invalides (Fig. 76), with its fine central feature. This is crowned by the most striking dome in Paris, one which takes rank as second only in Europe to our own St. Paul's, for beauty of form and appropriateness of treatment. The two domes are indeed somewhat alike in general outline.

The reign of Louis XIV. witnessed a large amount of building throughout France, as well as in the metropolis, and to the same period we must refer an enormous amount of lavish decoration in the interior of buildings, the taste of which is to our eyes painfully extravagant. Purer taste on the whole prevailed, if not in the reign of Louis XV. certainly in that of Louis XVI., to which period much really good decorative work, and some successful architecture belongs. The chief building of the latter part of the eighteenth century is the Pantheon (Ste. Geneviève), the best domed church in France, and one which must always take a high rank among Renaissance buildings of any age or country. The architect was Soufflot, and his ambition, like that of the old Gothic masons, was not only to produce a work of art, but a feat of skill; his design accordingly provided a smaller area of walls and piers compared with the total floor space than any other Renaissance church, or indeed than any great church, except a few of the very best specimens of late Gothic construction, such for example as King's College Chapel. The result has been that the fabric has not been quite stout enough to bear the weight of the dome, and that it has required to be tied and propped and strengthened in various ways from time to time. The plan of the Pantheon is a Greek cross, with a short vestibule, and a noble portico at the west, and a choir corresponding to the vestibule on the east. It has a fine central dome, which is excellently seen from many points of view externally, and forms the principal feature of the very effective interior. Each arm of the building is covered by a flat domical vault; a single order of pilasters and columns runs quite round the interior of the church occupying the entire height of the walls; and the light is admitted in a most successful manner by large semicircular windows at the upper part of the church, starting above the cornice of the order.

FIG. 76.—L'ÉGLISE DES INVALIDES, PARIS.

By J. H. Mansard. (Begun A.D. 1645.)

One other work of the eighteenth century challenges the admiration of every visitor to Paris and must not be overlooked, because it is at once a specimen of architecture and of that skilful if formal arrangement of streets and public places in combination with buildings which the French have carried so far in the present century. We allude to the two blocks of buildings, occupied as government offices, which front to the Place de la Concorde and stand at the corner of the Rue Royale. They are the work of Gabriel (1710-1782), and are justly admired as dignified if a little heavy and uninteresting. As specimens of architecture these buildings, with the Pantheon, are enough to establish a high character for French art at a time when in most other European countries the standard of taste had fallen to a very low level.

The hôtels (*i.e.* town mansions) and châteaux of the French nobility furnish a series of examples, showing the successive styles of almost every part of the Renaissance period. The phases of the style, subsequent to that of Francis the First, can however, be so well illustrated by public buildings in Paris, that it will be hardly necessary to go through a list of private residences however commanding; but the Château of Maisons, and the Royal Château of Fontainebleau, may be named as specimens of a class of building which shows the capacity of the Renaissance style when freely treated.

Renaissance buildings in France are distinguished by their large extent and the ample space which has been in many instances secured in connection with them. They are rarely of great height or imposing mass like the early Italian palaces. For the most part they are a good deal broken up, the surface of the walls is much covered by architectural features, not usually on a large scale, so that the impression of extent which really belongs to them is intensified by the treatment which their architects have adopted.

Orders are frequently introduced and usually correspond with the storeys of the building. However this may be the storeys are always well marked. The skyline also is generally picturesque and telling, though Versailles and the work of Lescot at the Louvre form an exception. Rustication is not much employed, and the vast but simple crowning cornices of the Italian palaces are never made use of. Narrow fronts like those at Venice, and open arcades or loggias like those of Genoa, do not form features of French Renaissance buildings; but on the other hand, much richness, and many varieties of treatment which the Italians never attempted, were tried, and as a rule successfully, in France.

Much good sculpture is employed in external enrichments, and a cultivated if often luxuriant taste is always shown. Many of the interiors are rich with carving, gilding, and mirrors, but harmonious coloured decoration is rare, and the fine and costly mosaics of Italy are almost unknown.

BELGIUM AND THE NETHERLANDS.

2. Belgium and the Netherlands

These countries afford but few examples of Renaissance. The Town Hall at Antwerp, an interesting building of the sixteenth century, and the Church of St. Anne at Bruges, are the most conspicuous buildings; and there are other churches in the style which are characteristic, and parts of which are really fine. The interiors of some of the town halls display fittings of Renaissance character, often rich and fanciful in the extreme, and bearing a general resemblance to French work of the same period.

FIG. 77.—WINDOW FROM COLMAR. (1575.)

FIG. 78.—ZEUGHAUS, DANTZIC. (1605.)

GERMANY AND NORTHERN EUROPE.

3. Germany

Buildings of pure Renaissance architecture, anterior to the nineteenth century, are scarce in Germany, or indeed in North-east Europe; but a transitional style, resembling our own Elizabethan, grew up and long held its ground, so that many picturesque buildings can be met with, of which the design indicates a fusion of the ideas and features of Gothic with those of classic art. This architectural style took so strong a hold that examples of it may be found throughout the seventeenth and eighteenth centuries in almost every northern town.

That part of the Castle of Heidelberg, which was built at the beginning of the seventeenth century, may be cited as belonging to this German transitional style. The front in this case is regularly divided by pilasters of the classic orders, but very irregular in their proportions and position. The windows are strongly marked, and with carved mullions. Large dormer windows break into the high roof; ornaments abound, and the whole presents a curiously blended mixture of the regular and the picturesque. Rather earlier in date, and perhaps rather more Gothic in their general treatment, are such buildings as the great Council Hall at Rothenberg (1572), that at Leipzig (1556), the Castle of Stuttgart (1553), with its picturesque arcaded quadrangle, or the lofty and elaborate Cloth Hall at Brunswick.

FIG. 79.—COUNCIL-HOUSE AT LEYDEN. (1599.)

Examples of similar character abound in the old inns of Germany and Switzerland, and many charming features, such as the window from Colmar (Fig. 77), dated 1575, which forms one of our illustrations could be brought forward. Another development of the same mixed style may be illustrated by the Zeug House at Dantzic (1605), of which we give the rear elevation (Fig. 78). Not altogether dissimilar from these in character is the finely-designed Castle of Fredericksberg at Copenhagen, testifying to the wide spread of the phase of architecture to which we are calling attention. The date of this building is 1610. A richer example, but one little if at all nearer to Italian feeling, is the Council House at Leyden, a portion of which we illustrate (Fig. 79). This building dates from 1599, and bears more resemblance to English Elizabethan in its ornaments, than to the architecture of any other country.

Simultaneously with these, some buildings made their appearance in Germany, which, though still picturesque, showed the dawn of a wish to adopt the features of pure Renaissance. The quadrangle of the Castle of Schalaburg (Fig. 80), may be taken as a specimen of the adoption of Renaissance ideas as well as forms. It is in effect an Italian cortile, though more ornate than Italian architects would have made it. It was built in the latter part of the sixteenth century, and seems to point to a wish to make use of the new style with but little admixture of northern ornament or treatment.

When architecture had quite passed through the transition period, which fortunately lasted long, the buildings, not only of Germany, but of the north generally, became uninteresting and tame; in fact, they present so few distinguishing features, that it is not necessary to describe or illustrate them. Russia, it is true, contains a few striking buildings belonging to the eighteenth century, but most of those which we might desire to refer to, were built subsequent to the close of that century.

FIG. 80.—QUADRANGLE OF THE CASTLE OF SCHALABURG.

(Late 16th Century.)

CHAPTER XIII.
RENAISSANCE ARCHITECTURE IN GREAT BRITAIN, SPAIN, AND PORTUGAL.

ENGLAND.—CHRONOLOGICAL SKETCH.

1. England. Chronological Sketch

IN England, as in France and Germany, the introduction of the Italian Renaissance was not accomplished without a period of transition. The architecture of this period is known as Elizabethan, though it lasted long after Elizabeth's reign. Sometimes it is called Tudor; but it is more convenient and not unusual to limit the term Tudor to the latest phase of English Gothic.

Probably the earliest introduction into any English building of a feature derived from the newly-revived classic sources is in the tomb of Henry VII. in Westminster Abbey. The grille inclosing this is of good, though late Gothic design; but when the tomb itself came to be set up, for which a contract was made with Torregiano in 1512, it was Italian in its details. The earliest examples of Renaissance features actually built into a structure, so far as we are aware, is in the terra-cotta ornamentation of Layer Marney House in Essex, which it is certain was erected prior to 1525. It is however long—surprisingly long—after this period before we come upon the traces of a general use of Renaissance details. In fact, up to the accession of Elizabeth (1558) they appear to have been little employed. It is however said that early in her reign the treatises on Renaissance architecture of Philibert de l'Orme and Lomazzo were translated from Italian into English, and in 1563 John Shute published a book on Italian architecture.

John of Padua, an Italian architect, was brought to this country by Henry VIII. and practised here; and Theodore Havenius of Cleves was employed as architect in the buildings of Caius College, Cambridge (1565-1574). These two foreigners undoubtedly played an important part in a change of taste which, though not general so early, certainly did commence before Elizabeth's death in 1603.

At the two universities, and in many localities throughout England, new buildings and enlargements of old ones were carried out during the long and prosperous reign of Elizabeth; and the style in which they were built will be found to have admitted of very great latitude. Where the intention was to obtain an effect of dignity or state, the classic principles of composition were more or less followed. The buildings at Caius College, Cambridge, Longleat, built between 1567 and 1579 by John of Padua, Woollaton, built about 1580 by Smithson, and Burleigh (built 1577), may be named as instances of this. On the other hand where a manorial or only a domestic character was desired, the main lines of the building are Gothic, but the details, in either case, are partly Gothic and partly modified Renaissance. This description will apply to such buildings as Knowle, Penshurst, Hardwick, Hatfield, Bramshill, or Holland House (Fig. 81). In the introductory chapter some account has been given, in general terms, of the features familiar to most and endeared to many, which mark these peculiarly English piles of buildings; those remarks may be appropriately continued here.

FIG. 81.—HOLLAND HOUSE AT KENSINGTON. (1607.)

The hall of Gothic houses was still retained, but only as one of a series of fine apartments. In many cases English mansions had no internal quadrangle, and are built as large solid blocks with boldly projecting wings. They are often of three storeys in height, the roofs are frequently of flat pitch, and in that case are hidden behind a parapet which is sometimes of fantastic design. Where the roofs are steeper and not concealed the gables are frequently of broken outline. Windows are usually very large, and with mullions and transoms, and it is to these large openings that Elizabethan interiors owe their bright and picturesque effects. Entrances are generally adorned with some classic or semi-classic features, often, however, much altered from their original model; here balustrades, ornamental recesses, stone staircases, and similar formal surroundings are commonly found, and are generally arranged with excellent judgment, though often quaint in design.

"This style is characterised by a somewhat grotesque application of the ancient orders and ornaments, by large and picturesquely-formed masses, spacious staircases, broad terraces, galleries of great length (at times 100 feet long), orders placed on orders, pyramidal gables formed of scroll-work often pierced, large windows divided by mullions and transoms, bay windows, pierced parapets, angle turrets, and a love of arcades. The principal features in the ornament are pierced scroll-work, strap-work, and prismatic rustication, combined with boldly-carved foliage (usually conventional) and roughly-formed figures." — M. D. W.

Interiors are bright and with ample space; very richly ornamented plaster ceilings are common; the walls of main rooms are often lined with wainscot panelling, and noble oak staircases are frequent.

In the reign of James I., our first Renaissance architect of mark, Inigo Jones (1572-1652) became known. He was a man of taste and genius, and had studied in Italy. He executed many works, the designs for which were more or less in the style of Palladio. These include the addition of a portico to the (then Gothic) cathedral of St. Paul's, and a magnificent design for a palace which Charles I. desired to build at Whitehall. A fragment of this building, now known as the Chapel Royal Whitehall, was erected, and small though it be, has done much by its conspicuous position and great beauty, to keep up a respect for Inigo Jones's undoubted high attainments as an artist.

More fortunate than Inigo Jones, Christopher Wren (1632-1723) had just attained a high position as a young man of science, skill, and cultivation, and as the architect of the Sheldonian Theatre at Oxford, when in 1666 the great fire of London destroyed the Metropolitan Cathedral, the parochial churches, the Royal Exchange, the Companies' Halls, and an immense mass of private property in London, and created an opportunity which made great demands upon the energy, skill, and fertility of design of the architect who might attempt to grasp it. Fortunately, Wren was equal to the occasion, and he has endowed London with a Cathedral which takes rank among the very foremost Renaissance buildings in Europe, as well as a magnificent series of parochial churches, and other public buildings. It is not pretended that his works are free from defects, but there can be no question that admitting anything which can be truly said against them, they are works of artistic genius, full of fresh and original design, and exhibiting rare sagacity in their practical contrivance and construction.

St. Paul's stands second only to St. Peter's as a great domical cathedral of Renaissance architecture. It falls far short of its great rival in actual size and internal effect, and is all but entirely devoid of that decoration in which St. Peter's is so rich. On the other hand, the exterior of St. Paul's (Fig. 82) is far finer, and as the English cathedral had the good fortune to be erected entirely from the plans and under the supervision of one architect, it is a building consistent with itself throughout, which, as we have seen, is more than can be said of St. Peter's.

The plan of St. Paul's is a Latin cross, with well marked transepts, a large portico, and two towers at the western entrance; an apse of small size forms the end of the eastern arm, and of each of the transepts; a great dome covers the crossing; the cathedral has a crypt raising the main floor considerably, and its side walls are carried high above the aisle roofs so as to hide the clerestory windows from sight.

The dome is very cleverly planted on eight piers instead of four at the crossing, and is a triple structure; for between the dome seen from within, and the much higher dome seen from without, a strong cone of brickwork rises which bears the weight of the stone lantern and ball and cross that surmount the whole. The skill with which the dome is made the central feature of a pyramidal composition whatever be the point of view, the great beauty of the circular colonnade immediately below the dome, the elegant outline of the western towers, and the unusual but successful distribution of the great portico, are among the most noteworthy elements which go to make up the charm of this very successful exterior.

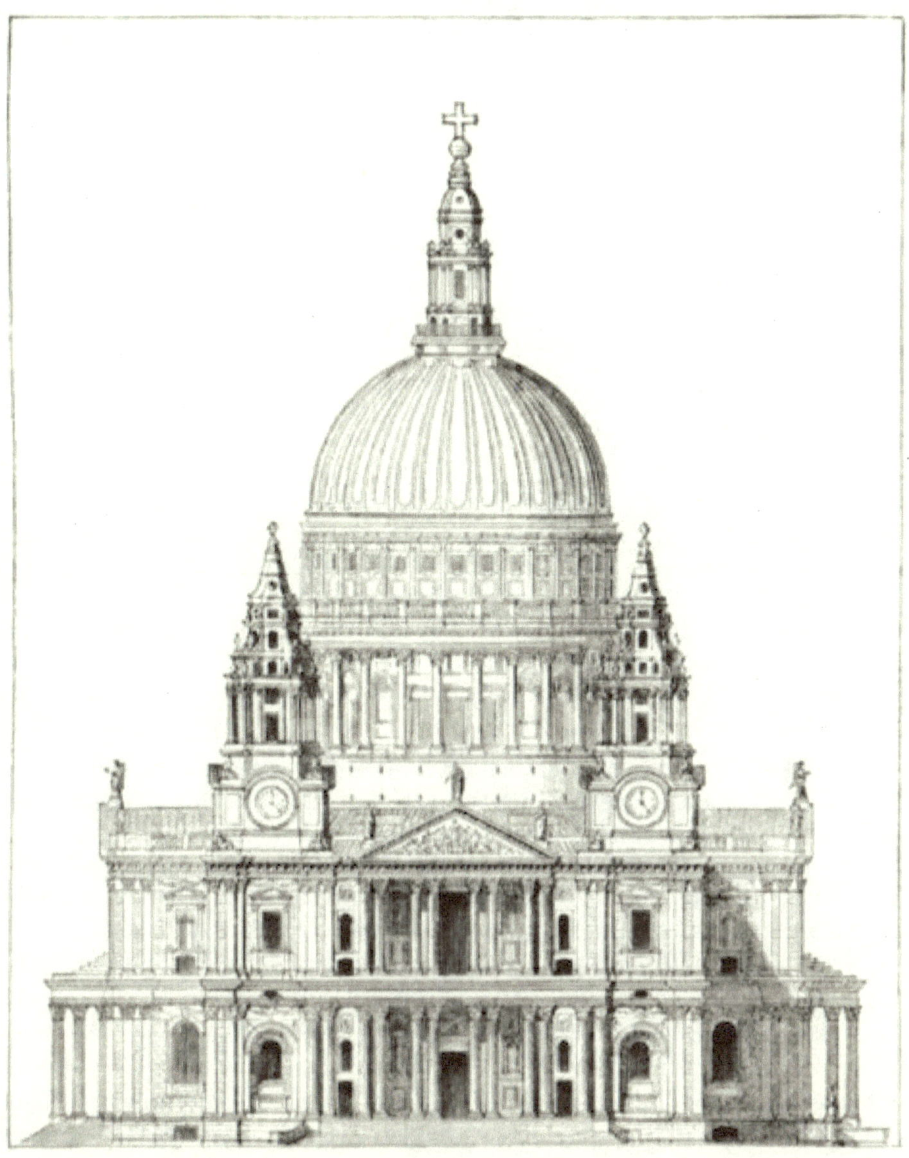

FIG. 82.—ST. PAUL'S CATHEDRAL, LONDON. (1675-1710.)

Wren may be said to have introduced to Renaissance architecture the tower and spire, for though many examples occur in Spain, there is reason to suppose that he was before the architects of that country in his employment of that feature. He has enriched the City of London with a large number of steeples, which are Gothic so far as their general idea goes, but thoroughly classic in details, and all more or less distinctive. The most famous of these is the one belonging to Bow Church; others of note belong to St. Clement Danes and St. Bride, Fleet Street.

The interiors of some of these churches, as for example St. Stephen, Walbrook, St. Andrew, Holborn, and St. James, Piccadilly, are excellent both for their good design and artistic treatment, and for their being well contrived and arranged for the special purposes they were intended to fill.

Wren's secular works were considerable. The Sheldonian Theatre at Oxford, the library of Trinity College, Cambridge, and the theatre of the College of Physicians London (long since disused), are a group of special buildings each of which was undoubtedly a remarkable and successful work. Chelsea and Greenwich hospitals are noteworthy as among the first specimens of those great buildings for public purposes in which England is now so rich, and which to a certain extent replace the monastic establishments of the middle ages. At Chelsea the building is simple and dignified. Without lavish outlay, or the use of expensive materials, much ornament, or any extraneous features, an artistic and telling effect has been produced, such as few hospitals or asylums since built have equalled. Greenwich takes a higher level, and though Wren's work had the disadvantage of having to be accommodated to buildings already erected by another architect, this building, with its twin domes, its rich outline, and its noble and dignified masses, will always reflect honour upon its designer. The view of Greenwich hospital from the river may fairly be said to be unique for beauty and picturesqueness. At Greenwich, too, we meet with some of that skill in associating buildings and open spaces together which is so much more common in France than in this country, and by the exercise of which the architecture of a good building can be in so many ways set off.

Wren, like Inigo Jones, has left behind him a great unexecuted design which in many respects is more noble than anything that he actually built. This is his earlier design for St. Paul's Cathedral, which he planned as a Greek cross, with an ampler dome than the present cathedral possesses, but not so lofty. A large model of this design exists. Had it been carried out the exterior of the building would probably not have appeared so commanding, perhaps not so graceful, as it actually is; but the interior would have surpassed all the churches of the style in Europe, both by the grandeur of the vast arched space under the dome and by the intricacy and beauty of the various vistas and combinations of features, for which its admirably-designed plan makes provision.

Wren had retired from practice before his death in 1723. His immediate successors were Hawksmoor, whose works were heavy and uninteresting, and Sir James Vanbrugh. Vanbrugh was a man of genius and has a style of his own, "bold, original, and pictorial." His greatest and best work is Blenheim, in Oxfordshire, built for the Duke of Marlborough. This fine mansion, equal to any French château in extent and magnificence, is planned with much dignity. The entrance front looks towards a large space, inclosed right and left by low buildings, which prolong the wings of the main block. The angles of the wings and the centre are masked by two colonnades of quadrant shape, and the central entrance with lofty columns which form a grand portico, is a noble composition.

The three garden fronts of Blenheim are all fine, and there is a magnificent entrance hall, but the most successful part of the interior is the library, a long and lofty gallery, occupying the entire flank of the house and treated with the most picturesque variety both of plan and ornament.

Vanbrugh also built Castle Howard, Grimesthorpe, Wentworth, King's Weston, as well as many other country mansions of more moderate size.

Campbell, Kent, and Gibbs are the best known names next in succession. Of these Campbell is most famous as an author, but Gibbs (1674-1754) is the architect of two prominent London churches—St. Martin's and St. Mary le Strand, in which the general traditions of Wren's manner are ably followed. He was the architect of the Radcliffe Library at Oxford. Kent (1684-1748) was the architect of Holkham, the Treasury Buildings, and the Horse Guards. He was associated with the Earl of Burlington, who acquired a high reputation as an amateur architect, which the design of Burlington House (now remodelled for the Royal Academy), went far to justify. Probably the technical part of this and other designs was supplied by Kent.

Sir William Chambers (1726-1796) was the architect of Somerset House, a building of no small merit, notwithstanding that it is tame and very bare of sculpture. This building is remarkable as one of the few in London in which the Italian feature of an interior quadrangle is attempted to be reproduced. Chambers wrote a treatise which has become a general text-book of revived classical architecture for English students. Contemporary with him were the brothers John and Robert Adam, who built much, and began to introduce a severity of treatment and a fineness of detail which correspond to some extent to the French style of Louis XVI. The interior decorations in plaster by these architects are of great elegance and often found in old houses in London, as in Hanover Square, on the Adelphi Terrace, and elsewhere. The list of the eighteenth century architects closes with the names of Sir Robert Taylor and the two Dances, one of whom built the Mansion House and the other Newgate; and Stuart, who built several country mansions, but who is best known for the magnificent work on the antiquities of Athens, which he and Revett published together in 1762, and which went far to create a revolution in public taste; for before the close of the century there was a general cry for making every building and every ornamental detail purely and solely Greek.

The architects above named, and others of less note were much employed during the eighteenth century in the erection of large country houses of Italian, usually Palladian design, many of them extremely incongruous and unsatisfactory. Here and there a design better than the average was obtained, but as a rule these stately but cold buildings are very far inferior to the picturesque and home-like manors and mansions built during the reigns of Elizabeth and James I.

FIG. 83.—HOUSES AT CHESTER. (16TH CENTURY.)

It is worth notice that the picturesque element, inherited from the Gothic architecture of the middle ages, which before the eighteenth century had completely vanished from our public buildings, and the mansions of the wealthy did not entirely die out of works executed in remote places. In the half-timbered manors and farmhouses which abound in Lancashire, Cheshire, Shropshire, and Staffordshire, and in other minor works, we always find a tinge, sometimes a very full colouring, of the picturesque and the irregular; the gables are sharp, upper storeys overhang, and the treatment of the timbers is thoroughly Gothic (Fig. 83); so are the mouldings, transoms and mullions to the windows, and barge boards to the roofs. In the reign of James I. a mode of enriching the exteriors of dwelling-houses, as well as their ceilings, chimney-pieces, &c., with ornaments modelled in plaster came in, and though the remaining specimens are from year to year disappearing, yet in some old towns (*e.g.* in Ipswich) examples of this sort of treatment (known as Jacobean) still linger.

In Queen Anne's reign a semi-Gothic version of Renaissance architecture was practised, to which great attention has been directed in the present day. The Queen Anne style is usually carried out in brickwork, executed in red bricks and often most admirable in its workmanship. Pilasters, cornices, and panels are executed in cut bricks, and for arches, niches, and window heads very finely jointed bricks are employed. The details are usually Renaissance, but of debased character; a crowning cornice of considerable projection under a high-pitched hipped roof (*i.e.* one sloping back every way like a truncated pyramid) is commonly employed; so also are gables of broken outline. Dormer windows rich and picturesque, and high brick chimneys are also employed; so are bow windows, often carried on concave corbels of a clumsy form. Prominence is given in this style to the joiner's work; the windows, which are usually sash windows, are heavily moulded and divided into small squares by wooded sash bars. The doors have heavily moulded panels, and are often surmounted by pediments carried by carved brackets or by pilasters; in the interiors the woodwork of staircases such as the balusters, newel posts, and handrails is treated in a very effective and well considered way, the greater part of the work being turned on the lathe and enriched with mouldings extremely well designed for execution in that manner. By this style and the modifications of it which were more or less practised till they finally died out, the traditional picturesqueness of English architecture which it had inherited from the middle ages was kept alive, so that it has been handed down, in certain localities almost, if not quite, to the present century.

SCOTLAND.

2. Scotland

The architecture of Scotland during the sixteenth and succeeding centuries possesses exceptional interest. It was the case here, as it had been in England, that the most important buildings of the time were domestic; the erection of churches and monasteries had ceased.

The castles and semi-fortified houses of Scotland form a group apart, possessing strongly-marked and well-defined character; they are designed in a mixed style in which the Gothic elements predominated over the classic ones. But the Scottish domestic Gothic, from which the new style was partly derived, had borne little or no resemblance to the florid Tudor of England. It was the severe and simple architecture of strongholds built with stubborn materials, and on rocky sites, where there was little inducement to indulge in decoration. Dunstaffnage or Kilchurn Castles may be referred to as examples of these plain, gloomy keeps with their stepped gables, small loops for windows, and sometimes angle turrets.

The classic elements of the style were not drawn (as had been the case in England) direct from Italy, but came from France. The Scotch, during their long struggles with the English, became intimately allied with the French, and it is therefore not surprising that Scottish Baronial architecture should resemble the early Renaissance of French châteaux very closely. The hardness of the stone in which the Scotch masons wrought forbade their attempting the extremely delicate detail of the François I. ornament, executed as it is in fine, easily-worked stone of smooth texture; and the difference in the climate of the two countries justified in Scotland a boldness which would have appeared exaggerated and extreme in France. Accordingly the style in passing from one country to the other has changed its details to no inconsiderable extent.

Many castles were erected in the sixteenth and following centuries in Scotland, or were enlarged and altered; the most characteristic features in almost all of them are short round angle turrets, thrown out upon bold corbellings near the upper part of towers and other square masses. These are often capped by pointed roofs; and the corbels which carry them, and which are always of bold, vigorous character, are frequently enriched by a kind of cable ornament, which is very distinctive. Towers of circular plan, like bastions, and projecting from the general line of the walls, or at the angles, constantly occur. They are frequently crowned by conical roofs, but sometimes (as at Fyvie Castle) they are made square near the top by means of a series of corbels, and finished with gables or otherwise. Parapets are in general use, and are almost always battlemented. Roofs, when visible, are of steep pitch, and their gables are almost always of stepped outline, while dormer windows, frequently of fantastic form, are not infrequent. Chimneys are prominent and lofty. Windows are square-headed, and, as a rule, small; sometimes they retain the Gothic mullions and transom, but in many cases these features are absent. Doorways are generally arched, and not often highly ornamented.

Cawdor Castle, Glamis Castle, Fyvie Castle, Castle Fraser, the old portions of Dunrobin Castle, Tyninghame House, the extremely picturesque palace at Falkland, and a considerable part of Stirling Castle, may be all quoted as good specimens of this thoroughly national style, but it would be easy to name two or three times as many buildings nearly, if not quite, equal to these in architectural merit.

Heriot's Hospital, Edinburgh, may be quoted (with part of Holyrood Palace) as showing the style of the seventeenth century. Heriot's Hospital was built between the years 1628 and 1660. It is built round a great quadrangle, and has square towers at the four corners, each relieved by small corbelled angle turrets. The entrance displays columns and an entablature of debased but not unpleasing Renaissance architecture, and the building altogether resembles an English Elizabethan or Jacobean building to a greater extent than most Scottish designs.

When this picturesque style, which appears indeed to have retained its hold for long, at last died out, very little of any artistic value was substituted for it. Late in the eighteenth century, it is true, the Brothers Adam erected public buildings in Edinburgh and Glasgow, and carried out various works of importance in a classic style which has certainly some claim to respect; but if correct it was tame and uninteresting, and a poor exchange for the vigorous vitality which breathes in the works of the architects of the early Renaissance in Scotland.

SPAIN AND PORTUGAL.

3. Spain and Portugal

In the Spanish peninsula, Renaissance architecture ran through three phases, very strongly distinguished from one another, each being marked by peculiarities of more than ordinary prominence. The early stage, to which the Spaniards give the name of Plateresco, exhibits the same sort of fusion of Gothic with classic which we find in France and Scotland. The masses are often simple, but the individual features are overladen with an extravagant amount of ornament, and, as in France, many things which are essentially Gothic, such as pinnacles, gargoyles, and parapets, are retained. The Renaissance style was introduced at the latter part of the fifteenth century, and a very considerable number of buildings to which the description given above will apply were erected prior to the middle of the sixteenth. Among these may be enumerated the cathedral at Granada, the Hospital of Santa Cruz at Toledo (1504-1514), the dome of Burgos Cathedral (1567), the Cathedral of Malaga, San Juan della Penitencia at Toledo (1511), the façade of the Alcazar at Toledo (1548), the Town Hall (1551), and Casa Zaporta (1560) at Zarragoza, and the Town Hall of Seville (1559).

A great number of tombs, staircases, doorways, and other smaller single features, executed during this period from the designs of good artists, are to be found scattered through the country. "These Renaissance monuments exhibit an extraordinary degree of variety in their ornaments, which are of the most fantastic nature; an exuberant fancy would seem to have sought a vent, especially in the sculptured ornament of the style, which though at times crowded, overladen, and we must add disfigured by the most grotesque ideas, is very striking for its originality and excellent workmanship." —(M. D. W.)

FIG. 84.—THE ALCAZAR AT TOLEDO. (BEGUN 1568.)

The second phase of Spanish architecture was marked by a plain and simple dignity, equally in contrast with the Plateresco which had preceded it and with the extravagant style to which it at length gave place. The earliest architect who introduced into Spain an architectural style founded on the best examples of Italy, was

Juan Baptista de Toledo. He in the year 1563 commenced the Escurial Palace—the Versailles of Spain; but the principal part of the building was erected by his more celebrated pupil, Juan de Herrera, who carried on the works during the years from 1567 to 1579. This building, one of the most extensive palaces in Europe, is noble in its external aspect from a distance, thanks to its great extent, its fine central dome, and its many towers, but it is disappointing when approached. Of the interior the most noteworthy feature is a magnificently decorated church, of great size and unusual arrangement; and this dignified central feature has raised the Escurial, in spite of many faults, to the position of the most famous and probably most deservedly admired among the great Renaissance palaces of Europe.

By the same architect numerous buildings were erected, among others the beautiful, if somewhat cold, arcaded interior of the Alcazar of Toledo (Fig. 84), which may be taken as a fair specimen of the noble qualities to be found in his dignified and comparatively simple designs. About the middle of the sixteenth century Charles V. erected his palace at Granada; but here the architecture is strongly coloured by Italian or French examples, and much of the building resembles Perrault's work at the Louvre very closely. Herrera and his school were probably too severe in taste to suit the fancy of their countrymen, for Spanish architecture in the eighteenth century fell a victim to debased forms and a fantastic and exaggerated style of ornament. Churriguera was the architect who has the credit of having introduced this unfortunate third manner, and has lent it his name. For a time "Churriguerismo" found general acceptance, and the century closed under its influence.

We must not pass over the excellent and varied Renaissance towers and steeples of Spain in silence. They are not unlike Wren's spires in general idea; they are to be met with in many parts of the country attached to the churches, and their variety and picturesqueness increase the claim of Spanish architecture to our respect.

The one Renaissance building in Portugal which has been much illustrated, and is spoken of in high terms, is the Convent at Mafra, a building of the eighteenth century, of great extent and picturesque effect. Great skill is shown in dealing with the unwieldy bulk of an overgrown establishment which does not yield even to the Escurial in point of extent. We are, however, up to the present time without the means of forming an opinion upon the nature and value of the architecture of Portugal as a whole.

INDEX

A

B

C

Lector House believes that a society develops through a two-fold approach of continuous learning and adaptation, which is derived from the study of classic literary works spread across the historic timeline of literature records. Therefore, we aim at reviving, repairing and redeveloping all those inaccessible or damaged but historically as well as culturally important literature across subjects so that the future generations may have an opportunity to study and learn from past works to embark upon a journey of creating a better future.

This book is a result of an effort made by Lector House towards making a contribution to the preservation and repair of original ancient works which might hold historical significance to the approach of continuous learning across subjects.

HAPPY READING & LEARNING!

LECTOR HOUSE LLP
E-MAIL: lectorpublishing@gmail.com

9 789389 701289